PEDIGREE DOGS

BOOK THREE

TERRIERS

*Official Standards
and
Colour Illustrations*

OTHER TITLES AVAILABLE
OR IN PREPARATION

20th Century Bulldog — by Marjorie Barnard
The Kennelgarth Scottish Terrier Book — by Betty Penn-Bull
The Bulldog — A Monograph by Edgar Farman
Keeshond of the World — by Margo Emerson
Staffordshire Bull Terrier in History and Sport — by Mike Homan
The Bullmastiff — by Clifford L.B. Hubbard
The Butterfly Dog — by Clarice Waud and Pat Chalice (limp)
The German Shepherd Dog — by Joyce Ixer
The Dalmation — by Clifford L.B. Hubbard
Toy Dogs — A Comprehensive Guide to Toy Dogs (HB) C. Waud
    and Mark Hutchings
Concise Guide to Dog Showing — by Paddy Petch (limp)
The Dog Book — by Betty Penn-Bull (limp)
Small Dog Obedience Training — by Mrs. R.A. Foreman (limp)
Bird Dogs of the World — Stanley .W.C. Smith

PEDIGREE DOGS IN COLOUR

BOOK THREE

TERRIERS

Roy Hodrien

Official Standards

*Colour Illustrations by
the Author*

NIMROD PRESS LTD

Dedicated to the memory of
Nan and Charlie

First Published in 1990

Pedigree Dogs in Colour   ISBN 1 85259 094 7

Book One – Hounds   ISBN 1 85259 205 2
Book Two – Gundogs   ISBN 1 85259 206 0
Book Three – Terriers   ISBN 1 85259 207 9
Book Four – Utility Group   ISBN 1 85259 208 7
Book Five – Working Group ISBN 1 85259 209 5
Book Six – Toy Group   ISBN 1 85259 210 9

NIMROD PRESS LTD
15 The Maltings
Turk Street
Alton, Hants, GU34 1DL

Produced by Jamesway Graphics
Middleton, Manchester

Printed in England

CONTENTS

Page

Acknowledgements   viii

BOOK ONE – **HOUNDS**

Afghan Hound   3
Basenji   6
Bassett Hound   9
Beagle   13
Bloodhound   16
Borzoi   20
Dachshund   23
Miniature Dachshund   30
Deerhound   35
Elkhound   39
Finnish Spitz   42
Greyhound   45
Ibizan Hound   48
Irish Wolfhound   51
Otterhound   54
Pharaoh Hound   58
Rhodesian Ridgeback   61
Saluki   65
Whippet   68

BOOK TWO – **GUNDOGS**

English Setter   73
German Shorthaired Pointer   76
Gordon Setter   80
Hungarian Vizsla   84
Irish Setter   87
Pointer   90
Curly-Coated Retriever   93
Flat-Coated Retriever   96
Golden Retriever   99
Labrador Retriever   102
American Cocker Spaniel   105

Clumber Spaniel 110
Cocker Spaniel 113
English Springer Spaniel 117
Field Spaniel 120
Irish Water Spaniel 123
Sussex Spaniel 126
Welsh Springer Spaniel 129
Weimaraner 132

BOOK THREE – **TERRIERS**

Airedale Terrier 139
Bedlington Terrier 143
Border Terrier 146
Bull Terrier 149
Bull Terrier (Miniature) 152
Cairn Terrier 154
Dandie Dinmount Terrier 157
Fox Terrier (Smooth and Wire) 161
Irish Terrier 167
Kerry Blue Terrier 171
Lakeland Terrier 174
Manchester Terrier 177
Norfolk Terrier 180
Norwich Terrier 183
Scottish Terrier 186
Sealyham Terrier 189
Skye Terrier 192
Soft-Coated Wheaten Terrier 195
Staffordshire Bull Terrier 199
Welsh Terrier 202
West Highland White Terrier 205

BOOK FOUR – **UTILITY GROUP**

Boston Terrier 211
Bulldog 215
Chow Chow 220
Dalmatian 223
French Bulldog 227
Japanese Spitz 230

Keeshond	233
Lhasa Apso	236
Miniature Schnauzer	239
Poodle	242
Schipperke	246
Schnauzer	249
Shih Tzu	253
Tibetan Spaniel	256
Tibetan Terrier	259

BOOK FIVE – **WORKING GROUP**

Bearded Collie	265
Belgian Shepherd Dog (Groenendael)	269
Belgian Shepherd Dog (Tervueren)	273
Bernese Mountain Dog	277
Border Collie	280
Bouvier des Flandres	283
Boxer	287
Briard	292
Bullmastiff	296
Rough Collie	300
Smooth Collie	304
Dobermann	308
The German Shepherd Dog	312
Giant Schnauzer	316
Great Dane	319
Komondor	323
Maremma Sheepdog	327
Mastiff	330
Newfoundland	333
Norwegian Buhund	337
Old English Sheepdog	340
Pyrenean Mountain Dog	343
Rottweiler	347
Saint Bernard	351
Samoyed	354
Shetland Sheepdog	357
Siberian Husky	361
Cardigan Welsh Corgi	365
Pembroke Welsh Corgi	368

BOOK SIX – **TOY GROUP**

Affenpinscher	373
Bichon Frise	376
Cavalier King Charles Spaniel	379
Chihuahua	382
Chinese Crested Dog	385
English Toy Terrier (Black and Tan)	388
Griffon Bruxellois	392
Italian Greyhound	395
Japanese Chin	398
King Charles Spaniel	401
Maltese	404
Miniature Pinscher	407
Papillon	410
Pekingese	414
Pomeranian	417
Pug	420
Yorkshire Terrier	423

ACKNOWLEDGEMENTS

My thanks are offered to all those who assisted with this book. In particular I acknowledge the role of the British Kennel Club who gave permission for the *Official Standards* to be reproduced. The American Club also kindly allowed me to quote from their *Standards* showing the main variations from the British Standards.

ROY HODRIEN

PEDIGREE DOGS IN COLOUR

BOOK THREE
TERRIERS

This is Book Three in a volume consisting of six books each dealing with a main group of dogs. The page numbering follows that used in the main volume.

Airedale Terrier
Bedlington Terrier

AIREDALE TERRIER

Easily the largest of the Terriers, the impressive Airedale possesses all the attributes of his smaller relatives in points of temperament, courage and hardiness.

He was bred around the mid 1800's and draws his name from the valley of Aire in Yorkshire where most of his development took place. Exactly which Terrier-types were involved in this breeding is not clear, but the Airedale's great size is thought to have come from the use of Otterhounds. In the formative years of the breed, it was known as the Waterside Terrier and an affinity with water is still to be seen in modern Airedales. Although these first specimens were far removed from the superbly proportioned dogs we see today, the foundations were laid for the breeders to build upon.

In Yorkshire the Airedale was widely used in vermin control and rats of any size were quickly exterminated with his powerful jaws. But since his official registration in 1886, the breed has been elevated above such unsavoury tasks and he is now a popular show dog. When trimmed and presented by an expert the Airedale will always create a lasting impression in a show-ring.

He makes a fine house dog, guarding his home with exteme forcefullness. With everyone in the family, though, the Airedale Terrier is friendly, co-operative and playful. He is not over-fond of his fellow dogs so on his exercise outings, which must be frequent, care should be taken to protect other people's pets.

```
┌─────────────────────────────────────────────────────────────┐
│                      KEY TO CHARACTER                        │
├─────────────────────────────────────────────────────────────┤
│                                                              │
│   INTELLIGENCE                              ****             │
│                                                              │
│   TEMPERAMENT                               ****             │
│                                                              │
│   EASE OF COAT CARE                         **               │
│                                                              │
│   SUITABILITY FOR                           *                │
│   SMALL DWELLING                                             │
│                                                              │
├─────────────────────────────────────────────────────────────┤
│                  ***** (5) = VERY GOOD                       │
└─────────────────────────────────────────────────────────────┘
```

BRITISH KENNEL CLUB STANDARD

AIREDALE TERRIER

CHARACTERISTICS. — Keen of expression, quick of movement, on the tip-toe of expectation at any movement. Character is denoted and shown by the expression of the eyes, and by the carriage of the ears and tail.

GENERAL APPEARANCE. — The various parts of the dog should be in proportion to each other giving a symmetrical appearance. In movement, the legs should be carried straight forward, the forelegs being perpendicular and parallel with the sides. The propulsive power is furnished by the hind legs, perfection of action being found in the Terrier possessing long thighs, and muscular second thighs well bent at the stifles, which admit of a strong forward thrust or snatch of the hocks. When approaching, the forelegs should form a continuatin of the straight line of the front, the feet being the same distance apart as the elbows; when stationary it is often difficult to determine whether a dog is slightly out at shoulder, but directly he moves, the defect if it exists, becomes most apparent, the forefeet having a tendency to cross. When, on the contrary, the dog is tied at the shoulder, the tendency of the feet is to move wider apart. When the hocks are turned in (cow-hocks) the stifles and feet are turned outward, resulting in a serious loss of propulsive power. When the hocks are turned outward, the tendency of the hind feet is to cross.

Head and Skull. — The skull should be long and flat, not too broad between the ears, and narrowing slightly to the eyes. It should be well balanced, with only little apparent difference in length between skull and foreface. The skull to be free from wrinkles, with stop hardly visible, and cheeks level and free from fullness. Foreface must be well filled up before the eyes, not dish-faced or falling away quickly below eyes, but on the other hand a little delicate chiselling should keep appearance from wedginess and plainness. Upper and lower jaws should be deep, powerful, strong and muscular, as strength of foreface is a great desideratum of the Airedale, but there must be no excess development of the jaws to give a rounded or bulging appearance to the cheeks, as "cheekiness" is not desired. Lips to be tight. The nose should be black.

Eyes. — Should be dark in colour, small, not prominent, full of terrier expression, keenness and intelligence.

Ears. — Should be "V" shaped with a side carriage, small, but not out of proportion to the size of the dog. The top line of the folded ear should be above the level of the skull. A pendulous ear, hanging dead by the side of the head like a hound's, is a fault.

Mouth. — Teeth strong and level being capable of closing together like a vice.

Neck. — Should be clean, muscular, of moderate length and thickness, gradually widening towards the shoulders, and free from throatiness.

Forequarters. — Shoulders should be long, well laid back, and sloping obliquely into the back, shoulder blades flat. Forelegs should be perfectly straight, with plenty of bone. Elbows should be perpendicular to the body, working free of the sides.

Body. — Back should be short, straight and level, with no appearance of slackness. Loins muscular. Ribs well sprung. In a well ribbed-up or short-coupled dog there is little space between ribs and hips. When the dog is long in couplings some slackness will be shown here. Chest to be deep but not broad.

Hindquarters. — Should be long and muscular with no droop. Thighs long and powerful with muscular second thigh, stifles well bent, not turned either in or out. Hocks well let down, parallel with each other when viewed form behind.

Feet. — Should be small, round and compact, with a good depth of pad, well cushioned, and the toes moderately arched, not turned either in or out.

Tail. — Should be set on high and carried gaily, but not curled over the back. It should be of good strength and substance, and of fair length.

Coat. — Should be hard, dense and wiry, and not too long as to appear ragged. It should also lie straight and close, covering the body and legs; the outer coat of hard, wiry, stiff hairs, the undercoat should be a shorter growth of softer hair. Some of the hardest coats are crinkling or just slightly waves; a curly coat is objectionable.

Colour. — The head and ears, with the exception of dark markings on each side of the skull, should be tan, the ears being of a darker shade than the rest. The legs up to the thighs and elbows also should be tan. The body to be black or dark grizzle.

Weight and Size. — Height about 23 inches to 24 inches for dogs, taken form top of shoulder, and bitches about 22 inches to 23 inches. Weight to be commensurate with height and type.

Note. — Male animals should have two apparently normal testicles fully descended into the scrotum.

MAIN AMERICAN KENNEL CLUB VARIATION TO STANDARD FOR THE AIREDALE TERRIER —

Size. — Dogs should measure approximately 23 inches in height at the shoulder; bitches slightly less.

AIREDALE TERRIER REGISTATIONS 1981 — 87 INCLUSIVE

1981 — 1383
1982 — 1327
1983 — 1356
1984 — 1401
1985 — 1369
1986 — 1454
1987 — 1238

CRUFTS BEST-IN-SHOW TWICE.

1961 CH. RIVERINA TWEEDSBAIRN — MISS P. McCAUGHEY AND MRS D. SCHUTH.
1986 CH. GINGER XMAS CAROL — MRS A. LIVRAGHI.

Border Terrier

BEDLINGTON TERRIER

Before 1825 this breed was referred to as the Rothbury Terrier after Rothbury Forest in Northumberland. It was there that gypsies kept dogs similar to todays Bedlington Terrier as pets and for small game hunting. In 1825 a dog enthusiast called Joseph Aynsley took a special interest in these dogs and intensive development was commenced. Aynsley re-named the breed after his home town of Bedlington.

The unique combination of this terrier's physical characteristics comes from Dandie Dinmont Terrier and Whippet blood. Two more different breeds you could not imagine, yet the Bedlington is a harmonious union of the Dandie Dinmont's toughness and attractive coat with the speed and agility of the Whippet. As a catcher of rats or rabbits there is none better than the fearless Bedlington Terrier and the working men of Northumberland used to exploit this talent to the full.

Around the home he conducts himself extremely well, being very easy to train and having a normally mild nature. When roused, however, the Bedlington shows great courage as a guard and will stand his ground against any man or animal who shows agression towards him.

A fair amount of varied exercise is needed to keep this athletic little dog well attuned both physically and mentally. To keep the thick coat clipped correctly does require a fair amount of work, although one advantage is that it does not shed.

KEY TO CHARACTER	
INTELLIGENCE	****
TEMPERAMENT	****
EASE OF COAT CARE	*
SUITABILITY FOR SMALL DWELLING	****
***** (5) = VERY GOOD	

BRITISH KENNEL CLUB STANDARD

BEDLINGTON TERRIER

GENERAL APPEARANCE. — A graceful, lithe, muscular dog, with no sign of either weakness or coarseness. The whole head should be pear or wedge-shaped, and expression in repose mild and gentle, though not shy or nervous. When roused, the eyes should sparkle and the dog look full of temper and courage. Bedlingtons are capable of galloping at great speed and should have the appearance of being able to do so. This action is very distinctive. Rather mincing, light and springy in the slower paces, could have slight roll when in full stride. When galloping must use the whole body.

Head and Skull. — Skull narrow, but deep and rounded; covered with profuse silky top-knot which should be nearly white. Jaw long and tapering. There must be no "stop," the line from occiput to nose end being straight and unbroken. Well filled up beneath the eye. Close fitting lips, without flew. The nostrils must be large and well-defined. Blues and blue-and-tans must have black noses; livers and sandies must have brown noses.

Eyes. — Small, bright and well sunk. The ideal eye has the appearance of being triangular. Blues should have a dark eye; blue-and-tans have lighter eyes with amber lights, and livers and sandies have a light hazel eye.

Ears. — Moderate sized, filbert shaped, set on low, and hanging flat to the cheek. They should be covered with short fine hair with a fringe of whiteish silky hair at the tip.

Mouth. — Teeth, level or pincer-jawed. The teeth should be large and strong.

Neck. — Long tapering neck, deep at the base; there should be no tendency to throatiness. The neck should spring well up from the shoulders, and the head should be carried rather high.

Forequarters. — The forelegs should be straight, but wider apart at the chest than at the feet. Pasterns long and slightly sloping without weakness. Shoulders flat and sloping.

Body. — Muscular, yet markedly flexible; flat-ribbed and deep through the brisket; well ribbed up. The chest should be deep and fairly broad. The back should be roached and the loin markedly arched. Muscular galloping quarters which are also fine and graceful.

Hindquarters. — Muscular and of moderate length. The hind legs, by reason of the roach back and arched loin, have the appearance of being longer than the forelegs. The hocks should be strong and well let down.

Feet. — Long hare feet with thick and well closed up pads.

Tail. — Of moderate length, thick at the root, tapering to a point and gracefully curved. Should be set on low, and must never be carried over the back.

Coat. — Very distinctive. Thick and linty, standing well out from the skin, but not wiry. There should be a distinct tendency to twist, particularly on the head and face.

Colour. — Blue, blue and tan, liver, or sandy. Darker pigment to be encouraged.

Weight and Size. — Height should be about sixteen inches at the shoulder. This allows of slight variation below in the case of a bitch and above in the case of a dog. Weight should be between eighteen and twenty-three pounds.

Note. — Male animals should have two apparently normal testicles fully descended into the scrotum.

MAIN AMERICAN KENNEL CLUB VARIATION TO STANDARD FOR THE BEDLINGTON TERRIER —

Height. — The preferred Bedlington Terrier dog measures 16½ inches at the withers, the bitch 15½ inches. Under 16 inches or over 17½ inches for dogs and under 15 inches or over 16½ inches for bitches are serious faults.

BEDLINGTON TERRIER REGISTRATONS 1981 — 87 INCLUSIVE

1981 — 200
1982 — 261
1983 — 157
1984 — 194
1985 — 198
1986 — 232
1987 — 217

YET TO WIN CRUFTS BEST-IN-SHOW.

BORDER TERRIER

Although diminutive in stature, the Border Terrier is far from being meek or fragile. He was bred from the hardy terriers that were native to the English/Scottish borderlands over a century ago. The goal of the men who began this breeding was to produce a compact yet speedy terrier who could keep pace with a fox hunt and who could stand his ground against a cornered badger. When used for fox hunting, the Border Terrier could make use of his size by burrowing through undergrowth to flush out the fox for his master's hounds. His very thick skin and hard, dense coat protected him well in this danger-frought activity. Modern breeders have endeavoured to maintain all his original characteristics and he is still kept by some of the hunting fraternity.

Since his registration over 60 years ago in Britain and subsequent recognition in the U.S.A., the Border Terrier has deservedly gathered a fair size following. He is a thoroughly genuine type with a first class dispositon and love of human company. He does not care for, or need, too much pampering but he will show great spirit and affection, especially if he is given plenty of outdoor exercise to work off his abundant energy. His size belies his guarding ability and he will defend his owner's home against all-comers.

KEY TO CHARACTER	
INTELLIGENCE	***
TEMPERAMENT	*****
EASE OF COAT CARE	*****
SUITABILITY FOR SMALL DWELLING	****
***** (5) = VERY GOOD	

BRITISH KENNEL CLUB STANDARD

BORDER TERRIER

CHARACTERISTICS. — The Border Terrier is essentially a working Terrier. It should be able to follow a horse and must combine activity with gameness.

Head and Skull. — Head like that of an otter, moderately broad in skull, with a short strong muzzle; a black nose is preferable but a liver or flesh-coloured one is not a serious fault.

Eyes. — Dark, with keen expression.

Ears. — Small, V-shaped, of moderate thickness and dropping forward close to the cheek.

Mouth. — Teeth should have a scissor-like grip, with the top teeth slightly in front of the lower, but level mouth is quite acceptable. An undershot or overshot mouth is a major fault and highly undesirable.

Neck. — Of moderate length.

Forequarters. — Forelegs straight and not too heavy in bone.

Body. — Deep and narrow and fairly long; ribs carried well back, but not over-sprung, as a terrier should be capable of being spanned by both hands behind the shoulder.

Hindquarters. — Racy. Loin strong.

Feet. — Small with thick pads.

Tail. — Moderately short and fairly thick at the base, then tapering, set high and carried gaily but not curled over the back.

Coat. — Harsh and dense with close undercoat. The skin must be thick.

Colour. — Red, wheaten, grizzle and tan or blue and tan.

Weight and Size. — Weight: Dogs, between 13 to 15½ lbs; Bitches, between 11½ to 14 lbs.

Note. — Male animals should have two apparently normal testicles fully descended into the scrotum.

BORDER TERRIER REGISTRATIONS 1981 — 87 INCLUSIVE

1981 — 1152
1982 — 1291
1983 — 1330
1984 — 1362
1985 — 1502
1986 — 1449
1987 — 1534

YET TO WIN CRUFTS BEST-IN-SHOW.

Bull Terrier

BULL TERRIER

The Bull Terrier first appeared in Britain in the mid-nineteenth century and owes his development to a breeder called James Hinks. Using the Old English White Terrier, The Bulldog and some believe the Dalmatian, he worked to perfect a dog that had the power of the Bulldog and the agility of the Terrier. As well as creating an attractive and popular breed, Hinks had produced the ultimate fighting dog, which in the nineteenth century was of great interest to the working classes. Organised dog fights were very popular and this new breed with a longer muzzle and greater speed than the other combatants, was invincible. When this dreadful pastime was abolished, the Bull Terrier's attractive appearance ensured that this was not the signal for his demise. He went on to become a hugely successful show-dog and although his heyday may have passed, he still takes many top honours all over the world.

Although the Bull Terrier can still be intolerant of other dogs, his behaviour with people is without fault. Even small children need have no fear of this gentle powerhouse. With firm training when young, he soon makes a clean, easily managed pet. It should be remembered, though, that a dog of such natural energy and stamina should be allowed plenty of free-running exercise and he will revel in long sessions of play.

As a guard of property he is awesome, any intruder being very foolish to dice with the great power of the Bull Terrier's jaws.

Although all early specimens where white, coloured Bull Terriers have existed for many years, brindle being the most popular. Deafness is a fairly common complaint in white puppies, so always check for this.

KEY TO CHARACTER	
INTELLIGENCE	***
TEMPERAMENT	****
EASE OF COAT CARE	*****
SUITABILITY FOR SMALL DWELLING	**
***** (5) = VERY GOOD	

BRITISH KENNEL CLUB STANDARD

BULL TERRIER

GENERAL APPEARANCE. — The Bull Terrier is the Gladiator of the canine race and must be strongly built, muscular, symmetrical and active, with a keen, determined and intelligent expression, full of fire and courageous but of even temperament and amenable to discipline. Irrespective of size, dogs should look masculine, and bitches feminine. Male animals should have two apparently normal testicles fully descended into the scrotum. The moving dog shall appear well-knit, smoothly covereing the ground with free easy strides and with a typical jaunty air. Fore and hind legs should move parallel each to each when viewed from in front or behind, the forelegs reaching out well and the hindlegs moving smoothly at the hip and flexing well at the stifle and hock with great thrust.

Head. — The head should be long, strong and deep, right to the end of the muzzle, but not coarse. Viewed from the front it should be egg-shaped and completely filled, its surface being free from hollows or indentations. The top of the skull should be almost flat from ear to ear. The profile should curve gently downwards from the top of the skull to the tip of the nose, which should be black and bent downwards at the tip. The nostrils should be well developed. The under-jaw should be strong.

Eyes. — The eyes should appear narrow, obliquely placed, and triangular, well sunken, black, or as dark brown as possible, so as to appear almost black, and with a piercing glint. The distance from the tip of the nose to the eyes should be perceptibly greater than that from the eyes to the top of the skull.

Ears. — The ears should be small, thin and placed close together. The dog should be able to hold them stiffly erect, when they should point straight upwards.

Mouth. — The teeth should be sound, clean, strong, of good size and perfectly regular. The upper front teeth should fit in front of and closely against the lower front teeth. The lips should be clean and tight.

Neck. — The neck should be very muscular, long, arched, tapering from the shoulders to the head, and free from loose skin.

Forequarters. — The shoulders should be strong and muscular but without loading. The shoulder blades should be wide, flat and attached closely to the chest wall, and should have a very pronounced backward slope of the front edge from bottom to top. The forelegs should have the strongest type of round quality bone and the dog should stand solidly upon them; they should be moderately long and perfectly parallel. The elbows should be held straight and the strong pasterns upright.

Body. — The body should be well rounded with marked spring of rib, and great depth from withers to brisket, so that the latter is nearer the ground than the belly. The back should be short and strong with the top line level behind the withers and arching or roaching slightly over the loin. The underline from brisket to belly should form a graceful upward curve. The chest should be broad viewed from the front.

Hindquarters. — The hindlegs should be in parallel viewed from behind. The thighs must be muscular and the second thigh well developed. The stifle joint should be well bent and the hock well angulated, with the bone to the foot short and strong.

Feet. — The feet should be round and compact with well arched toes.

Tail. — The tail should be short, set on low, it should be carried horizontally. Thick at the root it should taper to a fine point.

Coat. — The coat should be short, flat, even and harsh to the touch, with a fine gloss. The skin should fit the dog tightly.

Colour. — For white, pure white coat. Skin pigmentation and markings on the head should not be penalised. For coloured, the colour should predominate; all other things being equal, brindle to be preferred.

Weight and Size. — There are neither weight nor height limits but there should be the impression of the maximum of substance to the size of the dog.

Faults. — Any departure from the foregoing points should be considered a fault and the seriousness of the fault should be in exact proportion to its degree.
N.B. — Under Kennel Club Show Regulations, deafness is a disqualification.

BULL TERRIER REGISTRATIONS 1981 — 87 INCLUSIVE

1981 — 1426
1982 — 1626
1983 — 1676
1984 — 1965
1985 — 2178
1986 — 2263
1987 — 2532

CRUFTS BEST-IN-SHOW WINNER.

1972 CH. ABRAXAS AUDACITY — MISS V. DRUMMOND-DICK.

BULL TERRIER (MINIATURE)

The Miniature Bull Terrier is an exact scaled-down replica of the Bull Terrier. This type of Bull Terrier was developed simply by breeding from only the smallest specimens available. As the popularity of these dogs flourished in some quarters, so the breed was eventually established in it's own right.

All points relating to the Bull Terrier apply to the Miniature version and the standard differs only in the size and weight stipulatons.

Miniature Bull Terrier

KEY TO CHARACTER	
INTELLIGENCE	***
TEMPERAMENT	****
EASE OF COAT CARE	*****
SUITABILITY FOR SMALL DWELLING	*****
***** (5) = VERY GOOD	

BRITISH KENNEL CLUB STANDARD

BULL TERRIER (MINIATURE)

The standard of the Bull Terrier (Miniature) is the same as that of the Bull Terrier with the exception of the following:—

Weight and Size. — There should be an impression of the maximum of substance to the size of the dog. Height should not exceed 35cm (14″). The dog should at all times be balanced.

MINIATURE BULL TERRIER REGISTRATIONS 1981 — 87 INCLUSIVE

```
1981 —  65
1982 —  48
1983 —  49
1984 —  79
1985 —  65
1986 —  85
1987 — 124
```

YET TO WIN CRUFTS BEST-IN-SHOW.

Cairn Terrier
Dandie Dinmount Terrier

Smooth Fox Terrier
Wire Fox Terrier

CAIRN TERRIER

This is the breed from which all Scottish terriers are descended and he is one of the most ancient of all British terriers. It seems probable that the kennels which first developed the Cairn Terrier were on the Isle of Skye. The oldest of these kennels was a Captain MacLeod's who first bred these dogs approximately 150 years ago. These primitive Cairn Terriers were known as short-haired Skye Terriers until the official registration of the first Cairn in 1907. From then on he was developed steadily towards today's generally superior form.

His original use was as a hunter of small game and controller of vermin. Fox, badger, otter and rat being amongst his prey. He is ideally suited for this work due to his excellent burrowing ability. The Cairn's coat is well suited to the harsh conditions of his native environment, being hard, wiry and weather resistant.

He often lives to a good age and is basically hardy, confident, well balanced and fearless. The coat does not require too much attention, just an occassional brushing and he does not need lengthy periods of exercise to maintain his naturally fit and sturdy constitution. He has a lively and friendly nature, is never the neurotic type, and is loyal and amusing in the home. Both the elderly and young children alike will find the Cairn Terrier a commendable small dog.

KEY TO CHARACTER	
INTELLIGENCE	****
TEMPERAMENT	*****
EASE OF COAT CARE	****
SUITABILITY FOR SMALL DWELLING	*****
***** (5) = VERY GOOD	

BRITISH KENNEL CLUB STANDARD

CAIRN TERRIER

CHARACTERISTICS. — This terrier should impress with his fearless and gay disposition.

GENERAL APPEARANCE. — Active, game, hardy, and "shaggy" in appearance; strong, though compactly built. Should stand well forward on forepaws. Strong quarters, deep in ribs. Very free in movement. Coat hard enough to resist rain. Head small, but in proportion to body, a general foxy appearance is the chief characteristic of this working terrier.

Head and Skull. — Skull broad in proportion; strong, but not too long or heavy jaw. A decided indentation between eyes; hair should be full on forehead. Muzzle powerful but not heavy. Very strong jaw, which should be neither undershot nor overshot.

Eyes. — Set wide apart; medium in size; dark hazel, rather sunk, with shaggy eyebrows.

Ears. — Small, pointed, well carried and erect, but not too closely set.

Mouth. — Large teeth. Jaw strong and level.

Neck. — Well set on, but not short.

Forequarters. — Sloping shoulder and a medium length of leg; good, but not too large, bone. Forelegs should not be out at elbow. Legs must be covered with hard hair.

Body. — Compact, straight back; well sprung deep ribs; strong sinews. Back medium in length and well-coupled.

Hindquarters. — Very strong.

Irish Terrier
Kerry Blue Terrier

Lakeland Terrier
Manchester Terrier

Feet. — Forefeet, larger than hind, may be slightly turned out. Pads should be thick and strong. Thin and ferrety feet are objectionable.

Tail. — Short, well furnished with hair, but not feathery; carried gaily, but should not turn down towards back.

Coat. — Very important. Must be double-coated, with profuse, hard, but not coarse, outer coat, and undercoat which resembles fur, and is short, soft and close. Open coats are objectionable. Head should be well furnished.

Colour. — Red, sandy, grey, brindled, or nearly black. Dark points such as ears and muzzle, very typical.

Weight and Size. — Ideal weight, 14 lbs.

Faults. — Muzzle: undershot or overshot. Eyes: too prominent or too light. Ears: too large or round at points; they must not be heavily coated with hair. Coat: silkiness or curliness objectionable; a slight wave permissible. Nose: flesh or light coloured, most objectionable. In order to keep this breed to the best old working type, any resemblance to a Scottish Terrier will be considered objectionable.

Note. — Male animals should have two apparently normal testicles fully descended into the scrotum.

MAIN AMERICAN KENNEL CLUB VARIATION TO STANDARD FOR THE CAIRN TERRIER —

Ideal Size. — Weight for bitches, 13 pounds; for dogs, 14 pounds. Height at the withers — bitches, 9½ inches; dogs, 10 inches.

CAIRN TERRIER REGISTRATIONS 1981 — 87 INCLUSIVE

1981 — 2571
1982 — 2384
1983 — 2411
1984 — 2427
1985 — 2509
1986 — 2322
1987 — 2082

YET TO WIN CRUFTS BEST-IN-SHOW.

DANDIE DINMONT TERRIER

Not only is this breed unique in appearance, the origin of his name is also unusual. It is taken from a novel by Sir Walter Scott called "Guy Mannering", which features a character called Dandie Dinmont who keeps small terriers. Although the novel was published in 1814, it is thought that this breed goes back much further.

He first appeared in the early eighteenth century in the Scottish and English border counties. His ancestors were the various types of rough coated terriers of the region whose main function was the hunting of vermin. The early breeders wanted a low slung dog with sufficient burrowing ability to be able to easily root out badgers and foxes, amongst other prey. The long body could possibly come from the use of dogs similar to the Skye Terrier we know today and other suggestions of breeds used to formulate the modern Dandie Dinmont are the Dachsund and the Otterhound.

Although the Dandie Dinmont is not one of the most popular breeds with the general public, he has many good qualities. The relatively small number being bred has helped to keep a strong blood line and his courage and faithfullness have remained firmly implanted in his character. He is a very confident dog, a good guard whilst also being playful and patient. The attractive top-knot and the rest of the Dandie Dinmont's coat does require care to maintain the best appearance. Exercise should be brisk and very frequent.

Norfolk Terrier
Norwich Terrier

Scottish Terrier
Sealyham Terrier

KEY TO CHARACTER	
INTELLIGENCE	***
TEMPERAMENT	****
EASE OF COAT CARE	**
SUITABILITY FOR SMALL DWELLING	****
***** (5) = VERY GOOD	

BRITISH KENNEL CLUB STANDARD

DANDIE DINMONT TERRIER

Head and Skull. — Head strongly made and large, not out of proportion to the dog's size, the muscles showing extraordinary development, more especially the maxillary. Skull broad between the ears, getting gradually less towards the eye, and measuring about the same from the inner corner of the eye to back of skull as it does from ear to ear. The forehead well domed. The head is covered with very soft silky hair, which should not be confined to a mere top-knot, and the lighter in colour and silkier it is the better. The cheeks, starting from the ears proportionately with the skull, have a gradual taper towards the muzzle, which is deep and strongly made, and measures about three inches in length, or in proportion to skull as three is to five. The muzzle is covered with hair of a little darker shade than top-knot, and of the same texture as the feather of the forelegs. The top of the muzzle is generally bare for about an inch from the back part of the nose, the bareness coming to a point towards the eye, and being about one inch broad at the nose. The nose black.

Eyes. — Set wide apart, large, full, round but not protruding, bright, expressive of great determination, intelligence, and dignity, set low and prominent in front of the head, colour, a rich dark hazel.

Ears. — Pendulous, set well back wide apart and low on the skull, hanging close to the cheek, with a very slight projection at the base, broad at the junction of the head and tapering almost to a point, the for part of the ear coming almost straight down from its junction with the head to the tip. They shall harmonise in colour with the body colour. In the case of a pepper dog they are covered with a soft, straight, dark hair (in some cases almost black). In the case of a mustard dog, the hair should be mustard in colour, a shade darker than the body, but not black. All should have a thin feather of light hair starting about two inches from the tip, and of nearly the same colour and texture as the top-knot, which give the ear the appearance of a distinct point. The animal is often one or two years old before the feather is shown. The cartilage and skin of the ear should not be thick, but very thin. Lengh of ear, from three to four inches.

Mouth. — The inside of the mouth should be black or dark coloured. The teeth very strong, especially the canine, which are of extraordinary size for such a small dog. The canines fit well into each other, so as to give the greatest available holding and punishing power, and the teeth are level in front, the upper ones very slightly overlapping the under ones. Undershot or overshot mouths are equally objectionable.

Neck. — Very muscular, well developed, and strong, showing great power of resistance, being well set into the shoulders.

Forequarters. — The forelegs short, with immense muscular development and bone, set wide apart and chest coming well down between them. Bandy legs are objectionable. The hair on the forelegs of a pepper dog should be tan, varying according to the body colour from a rich tan to a pale fawn; of a mustard dog they are of a darker shade than its head, which is a creamy white. In both colours there is a nice feather about two inches long, rather lighter in colour than the hair on the fore part of the leg.

Body. — Long, strong, and flexible; ribs well sprung and round, chest well developed and let down between the forelegs; the back rather low at the shoulders having a slight downward curve and a corresponding arch over the loins, with a very slight gradual drop from top of loin to root of tail; both sides of backbone well supplied with muscle.

Hindquarters. — The hind legs are a little longer than the fore ones, and are set rather wide apart, but not spread out in an unnatural manner; the thighs are well developed, and the hair of the same colour and texture as the fore ones, but having no feather or dew claws.

Feet. — Flat feet are objectionable. The whole claws should be dark, but the claws of all vary in shade according to the colour of the dog's body. The feet of a pepper dog should be tan, varying according to the body colour from a rich tan to a pale fawn; of a mustard dog they are a darker shade than its head. Hind feet should be much smaller than the fore feet.

Tail. — Rather short, say from eight to ten inches, and covered on the upper side with wiry hair of a darker colour than that of the body, the hair on the under side being lighter in colour, and not so wiry, with a nice feather about two inches long, getting shorter as it nears the tip; rather thick at the root, getting thicker for about four inches, then tapering off to a point. It should not be twisted or curled in any way, but should come up with a curve like a scimitar, the tip, when excited, being in a perpendicular line with the root of the tail. It should neither be set too high nor too low. When not excited it is carried gaily, and a little above the level of the body.

Coat. — This is a very important point. The hair should be about two inches long; that from the skull to root of tail a mixture of hardish and soft hair, which gives a sort of crisp feel to the hand. The hard should not be wiry; the coat is what is termed pily or pencilled. The hair on the under part of the body is lighter in colour and softer than that on the top. The skin on the belly accords with the colour of the dog.

Colour. — The colour is pepper or mustard. The pepper ranges from a dark bluish black to a light silvery grey, the intermediate shades being preferred, the body colour coming well down the shoulder and hips, gradually merging into the leg colour. The mustards vary from a reddish brown to a pale fawn, the head being a creamy white, the legs and feet of a shade darker than the head. The claws are dark as in other colours. (Nearly all Dandie Dinmont Terriers have some white on the chest, and some have white claws.) White feet are objectionable.

Skye Terrier
Soft-Coated Wheaten Terrier

Staffordshire Bull Terrier
Welsh Terrier

Weight and Size. — The height should be from eight to eleven inches at the top of shoulder. Length from top of shoulder to root of tail should not be more than twice the dog's height, but, preferably, one or two inches less. The ideal weight as near eighteen pounds as possible. This weight is for dogs in good working order.

Note. — Male animals should have two apparently normal testicles fully descended into the scrotum.

MAIN AMERICAN KENNEL CLUB VARIATION TO STANDARD FOR THE DANDIE DINMONT TERRIER —

Weight. — The preferred weight from 18 to 24 pounds. These weights are for dogs in good working condition.

DANDIE DINMONT TERRIER REGISTRATIONS 1981 — 87 INCLUSIVE

1981 — 204
1982 — 154
1983 — 130
1984 — 184
1985 — 149
1986 — 204
1987 — 190

YET TO WIN CRUFTS BEST-IN-SHOW.

West Highland White Terrier

FOX TERRIER (SMOOTH AND WIRE)

The Fox Terrier as we know him today was developed purely for hunting purposes. Fox hunting enthusiasts of the early eighteenth century required a dog that was small and sturdy enough to burrow for foxes and was also long enough in the leg to keep up with a fast-paced hunt. The Beagle and Foxhound are likely to have been included in his production and the predominantly white coat was probably obtained from the introduction of Bull Terrier blood. This white colouration was an aid to the hunter as many darker terriers had been mistaken for the fox and attacked by the hounds.

The Smooth and Wire Fox Terriers are of identical origin with the coat being their only distinguishing feature. The Smooth Fox Terrier was undoubtedly the more popular of the two up until the start of this century. It was then that the Wire haired gradually became the more sought after, this being mainly due to development in coat care techniques which helped greatly with maintenance.

The Fox Terrier is a very manageable breed.in the home, enjoying human companionship and standing no nonsense from potential intruders. They are very alert and sharp in reaction but never nervous or unpredictable. The more dense and hard the coat of the Wire Fox Terrier, the better and it should be given plenty of attention to avoid scruffiness. As he was bred for stamina when hunting, the Fox Terrier must have regular vigorous exercise.

KEY TO CHARACTER		
INTELLIGENCE		***
TEMPERAMENT		****
EASE OF COAT CARE	SMOOTH WIRE	***** **
SUITABILITY FOR SMALL DWELLING		***
***** (5) = VERY GOOD		

BRITISH KENNEL CLUB STANDARD

FOX TERRIER (SMOOTH)

GENERAL APPEARANCE. — The dog must present a general gay, lively, and active appearance; bone and strength in a small compass are essentials, but this must not be taken to mean that a Fox Terrier should be cloggy, or in any way coarse, speed and endurance must be looked to as well as power, and the symmetry of the Foxhound taken as a model. The Terrier, like the Hound, must on no account be leggy, nor must he be too short in the leg. He should stand like a cleverly made Hunter, covering a lot of ground, yet with a short back. He will then attain the highest degree of propelling power, together with the greatest length of stride that is compatible with the length of his body.

Head and Skull. — The skull should be flat and moderately narrow, and gradually decreasing in width to the eyes. Not much "stop" should be apparent, but there should be more dip in the profile between the forehead and the top jaw than is seen in the case of the Greyhound. The cheeks must not be full. The jaw, upper and under, should be strong and muscular, should be of fair punishing strength, but not so in any way to resemble the Greyhound. There should not be much falling away below the eyes. This part of the head should, however, be moderately chiselled out, so as not to go down in a straight line like a wedge. The nose, towards which the muzzle must gradually taper, should be black.

Eyes. — Should be dark in colour, small and rather deep set, full of fire, life, and intelligence; as nearly as possible circular in shape.

Ears. — Should be V-shaped and small, of moderate thickness, and dropping forward close to the cheek, not hanging by the side of the head like a Foxhound's.

Mouth. — The teeth should be nearly as possible level, i.e., the upper teeth on the outside of the lower teeth.

Neck. — Should be clean and muscular, without throatiness, of fair length, and gradually widening to the shoulders.

Forequarters. — The shoulders should be long and sloping, well laid back, fine at the points, and clearly cut at the withers.

Body. — Chest deep and not too broad. Back should be short, straight and strong, with no appearance of slackness. Loin should be powerful and very slightly arched. The fore ribs should be moderately arched, the back ribs deep; and the dog should be well ribbed up.

Hindquarters. — Should be strong and muscular, quite free from droop or crouch; the thighs long and powerful; hocks near the ground, the dog standing well up on them like a Foxhound, and not straight in stifle.

Feet. — Should be round, compact and not large. The soles hard and tough. The toes moderately arched, and turned neither in nor out.

Tail. — Should be set on rather high, and carried gaily, but not over the back nor curled. It should be of good strength.

Coat. — White should predominate; brindle, red or liver markings are objectionable. Otherwise this point is of litle or no importance.

Weight and Size. — Weight is not a certain criterion of a Terrier's fitness for his work — general shape, size and contour are the main points — and if a dog can gallop and stay, and follow his fox up a drain, it matters little what his weight is to a pound or so, though, roughly speaking, 15 to 17 lbs. for a bitch and 16 to 18 lbs. for a dog in Show condition are appropriate weights.

Faults. — Nose, white, cherry, or spotted to a considerable extent with either of these colours. Ears, prick, tulip or rose. Mouth, much undershot or much overshot.

Note. — Male animals should have two apparently normal testicles fully descended into the scrotum.

MAIN AMERICAN KENNEL CLUB VARIATION TO STANDARD FOR THE SMOOTH FOX TERRIER —

Size. — According to present-day requirements, a full-sized well-balanced dog should not exceed 15½ inches at the withers.

SMOOTH FOX TERRIER REGISTRATIONS 1981 — 87 INCLUSIVE

1981 — 316
1982 — 308
1983 — 318
1984 — 305
1985 — 319
1986 — 251
1987 — 344

YET TO WIN CRUFTS BEST-IN-SHOW.

FOX TERRIER (WIRE)

CHARACTERISTICS. — The Terrier should be alert, quick of movement keen of expression, on the tip-toe of expectation at the slightest provocation. Character is imparted by the expression of the eyes and by the carriage of ears and tail.

GENERAL APPEARANCE. — The dog should be balanced and this may be defined as the correct proportions of a certain point or points, when considered in relation to a certain other point or points. It is the keystone of the Terrier's anatomy. The chief points for consideration are the relative proportions of skull and foreface; head and back; height at withers; and length of body from shoulder-point to buttock — the ideal of proportion being reached when the last two measurements are the same. It should be added that, although the head measurements can be taken with absolute accuracy, the height at withers and length of back are approximate, and are inserted for the information of breeders and exhibitors rather than as a hard-and-fast rule. The movement or action is the crucial test of conformation. The Terrier's legs should be carried straight forward while travelling, the forelegs hanging perpendicular and swinging parallel to the sides, like the pendulum of a clock. The principal propulsive power is furnished by the hind legs, perfection of action being found in the Terrier possessing long thighs and muscular second-thighs well bent at the stifles, which admit of a strong forward thrust or "snatch" of the hocks. When approaching the forelegs should form a continuation of the straight of the front, the feet being the same distance apart as the elbows. When stationary it is often difficult to determine whether a dog is slightly out at shoulder but directly he moves the defect — if it exists — becomes more apparent, the fore-feet having a tendency to cross, "weave" or "dish". When on the contrary, the dog is tied at the shoulder, the tendency of the feet is to move wider apart, with a sort of padding action. When the hocks are turned in — cow hocks — the stifles and feet are turned outwards, resulting in a serious loss of propulsive power. When the hocks are turned outwards the tendency of the hind feet is to cross, resulting in an ungainly waddle.

Head and Skull. — The top line of the skull should be almost flat, sloping slightly and gradually decreasing in width towards the eyes. In a well-balanced head there should be little apparent difference in length between skull and foreface. If, however, the foreface is noticeably shorter, it amounts to a fault, the head looking weak and "unfinished". On the other hand, when the eyes are set too high up in the skull, and too near the ears, it also amounts to a fault, the head being said to have a "foreign appearance". Although the foreface should gradually taper from eye to muzzle and should dip slightly at its juncture with the forehead, it should not "dish" or fall away quickly below the eyes, where it should be full and well made up, but relieved from "wedginess" by a little delicate chiselling. While well-developed jaw bones, armed with a set of strong white teeth, impart that appearance of strength to the foreface which is desirable. An excessive bony or muscular development of the jaws is both unnecessary and unsightly, as it is partly responsible for the full and rounded contour of the cheeks to which the term "cheeky" is applied. Nose should be black.

Eyes. — Should be dark in colour, moderately small and not prominent, full of fire, life, and intelligence; as nearly as possible, circular in shape and not too far apart. Anything approaching a yellow eye is most objectionable.

Ears. — Should be small and V-shaped and of moderate thickness, the flaps neatly folded over and drooping forward close to the cheeks. The top line of the folded ear should be well above the level of the skull. A pendulous ear, hanging dead by the side of the head like a hound's is uncharacteristic of the Terrier, while an ear which is semi-erect is still more undesirable.

Mouth. — Both upper and lower jaws should be strong and muscular, the teeth as nearly as possible level and capable of closing together like a vice — the lower canines locking in front of the upper and the points of the upper incisors slightly overlapping the lower.

Neck. — Should be clean, muscular, of fair length, free from throatiness and presenting a graceful curve when viewed from the side.

Forequarters. — Shoulders when viewed from the front, should slope steeply downwards from their juncture, with the neck towards the points, which should be fine. When viewed from the side they should be long, well laid back, and should slope obliquely backwards from points to withers, which should always be clean cut. A shoulder well laid back gives the long fore-hand, which, in combination with a short back, is so desirable in Terrier or Hunter. Chest deep and not broad, a too narrow chest being almost as undesirable as a very broad one. Excessive depth of chest and brisket is an impediment to a Terrier when going to ground. Viewed from any direction the legs should be straight, the bone of the forelegs strong right down to the feet. The elbows should hang perpendicular to the body, working free of the sides, carried straight through in travelling.

Body. — The back should be short and level, with no appearance of slackness — the loins muscular and very slightly arched. The brisket should be deep, the front ribs moderately arched, and the back ribs deep, and well sprung. The term "slackness" is applied both to the portion of the back immediately behind the withers when it shows any tendency to dip, and also the flanks when there is too much space between the back-ribs and hip-bone. When there is little space between the ribs and hips, the dog is said to be "short in couplings", "short-coupled", or "well-ribbed up". A Terrier can scarcely be too short in back, provided he has sufficient length of neck and liberty of movement. The bitch may be slightly longer in couplings than the dog.

Hindquarters. — Should be strong and muscular, quite free from droop or crouch; the thighs long and powerful; the stifles well curved and turned neither in nor out; the hock-joints well bent and near the ground; the hocks perfectly upright and parallel with each other when viewed from behind. The worst possible form of hindquarters consists of a short second-thigh and a straight stifle, a combination which causes the hind-legs to act as props rather than instruments of propulsion. The hind-legs should be carried straight through in travelling.

Feet. — Should be round, compact, and not large — the pads tough and well cushioned, and the toes moderately arched and turned neither in nor out. A Terrier with good-shaped fore-legs and feet will wear his nails down short by contact with the road surface, the weight of the body being evenly distributed between the toe-pad and the heels.

Tail. — Should be set on rather high and carried gaily but not curled. It should be of good strength and substance and of fair length — a three-quarter dock is about right — since it affords the only safe grip when handling working Terriers. A very short tail is suitable neither for work nor show.

Coat. — The principal difference between that of the Smooth and Wire variety is that, whereas the former is straight and flat, that of the latter appears to be broken — the hairs having a tendency to twist. The best coats are of a dense, wiry texture — like cocoa-nut matting — the hairs growing so closely and strongly together that when parted with the fingers the skin cannot be seen. At the base of these stiff hairs is a shorter growth of finer and softer hair — termed the under coat. The coat on the sides is never quite so hard as that on the back and quarters. Some of the hardest coats are "crinkly" or slightly waved, but a curly coat is very objectionable. The hair on the upper and lower jaws should be crisp and only sufficiently long to impart an appearance of strength to the fore-face, thus effectually differentiating them from the Smooth variety. The hair on the fore-legs should also be dense and crisp. The coat should average in length from ¾ to 1 inch on shoulders and neck, lengthening to 1½ inches on withers, backs, ribs and quarters. These measurements are given rather as a guide to exhibitors than as an infallible rule, since the length of coat varies in different specimens and seasons. The judge must form his own opinion as to what constitutes a "sufficient" coat.

Colour. — White should predominate: brindle, red, liver, or slaty blue are objectionable. Otherwise, colour is of little or no importance.

Weight and Size. — Bone and strength in a small compass are essential, but this must not be taken to mean that a Terrier should be "cloddy", or in any way coarse — speed and endurance being requisite as well as power. The Terrier must on no acount be leggy, nor must he be too short on the leg. He should stand like a cleverly-made, short-backed Hunter, covering a lot of ground. According to present-day requirements, a full-sized, well-balanced dog should not exceed 15½ inches at the withers — the bitch being proportionately lower — nor should the length of back from withers to root of tail exceed 12 inches, while to maintain the relative proportions, the head — as before mentioned — should not exceed 7¼ inches or be less than 7 inches. A dog with these measurements should scale 18 lbs. in show condition — a bitch weighing some 2 lbs. less — with a margin of 1 lb. either way.

Faults. — Nose: white, cherry, or spotted to a considerable extent with either of these colours. Ears: prick, tulip, or rose. Mouth: much undershot or much overshot.

N.B. — Old scars or injuries, the result of work or accident, should not be allowed to prejudice a Terrier's chance in the show-ring, unless they interfere with its movement or with its utility for work or stud.

Note. — Male animals should have two apparently normal testicles fully descended into the scrotum.

WIRE FOX TERRIER REGISTRATIONS 1981 — 87 INCLUSIVE

1981 — 738
1982 — 677
1983 — 681
1984 — 681
1985 — 747
1986 — 661
1987 — 656

CRUFTS BEST-IN-SHOW WINNER 3 TIMES.

1962 CH. CRACKWYN COCKSPUR — H.L. GILL
1975 CH. BROOKEWIRE BRANDY OF LAYVEN — MESSRS. BENELLI AND DONDINA
1978 CH. HARROWHILL HUNTSMAN — MISS E. HOWLES.

IRISH TERRIER

At first glance this ancient breed from the Emerald Isle looks like a scaled-down Airedale or an over-blown Lakeland Terrier. But apart from the colour difference the Irish Terrier has a unique head and a conformation all of his own.

Much legend and uncertainty surrounds the breed's beginnings, some Irishmen even maintaining that he is a close relation of the Irish Wolfhound. But in all corners of the Britissh Isles small wire-haired hunting terriers have existed for centuries and Ireland is no exception. So it would seem very probable that the Irish Terrier is from stock of this sort, and his efficiency as a ratter and catcher of small game adds weight to that idea.

Until the late 1870's when the breed became more standardised, the colouring had varied quite widely. Now the colours of bright red, red wheaten or yellow red are insisted upon by the breed standard.

As might be expected of a true Terrier, expecially an Irish one, he is full of spirit, mischief and courage. He has gained, rather unfairly, a reputation as a vicious fighter, but whilst he will take no nonsense from any dog, he will normally mind his own business.

He is easily trained for the home and is naturally adaptable to any environment that his owner lives in. Children will enjoy his company and if exercised regularly he makes a high-spirited, good-natured companion.

KEY TO CHARACTER	
INTELLIGENCE	****
TEMPERAMENT	****
EASE OF COAT CARE	***
SUITABILITY FOR SMALL DWELLING	***
***** (5) = VERY GOOD	

BRITISH KENNEL CLUB STANDARD

IRISH TERRIER

CHARACTERISTICS. — Dogs that are very game are usually surly or snappish. The Irish Terrier as a breed is an exception, being remarkably good tempered, notably so with humans, it being admitted, however, that he is perhaps a little too ready to resent interference on the part of other dogs. There is a heedless, reckless pluck about the Irish Terrier which is characteristic, and coupled with the head-long dash, blind to all consequence, with which he rushes at his adversary, has earned for the breed the proud epithet of "The Dare Devils". When "off duty" they are characterised by a quiet caress-inviting appearance, and when one sees them endearingly, timidly pushing their heads into their master's hands, it is difficult to realise that on occasions, at the "set on", they can prove that they have the courage of a lion, and will fight unto the last breath in their bodies. They develop an extraordinary devotion for, and have been known to track their masters almost incredible distances.

GENERAL APPEARANCE. — The dog must present an active, lively, lithe and wiry appearance; with lots of substance, at the same time free of clumsiness, as speed and endurance, as well as power, are very essential. They must be neither "cloddy" nor "cobby", but should be framed on the "lines of speeds", showing a graceful "racing outline".

Head and Skull. — Head long; skull flat, and rather narrow between ears, getting slightly narrower trowards the eye; free from wrinkles; stop hardly visible except in profile. The jaw must be strong and muscular, but not too full in the cheek, and of a good punishing length. The foreface should not "dish" or fall away quickly between or below the eyes, where it should be well made up, being relieved of "wedginess" by delicate chiselling. The hiar should be crisp and only sufficiently long to impart an appearance of additional strength to the foreface. Lips should be well fitting and externally almost black in colour. The nose must be black.

Eyes. — A dark colour, small not prominent, and full of life, fire and intelligence. A light or yellow eye is a fault.

Ears. — Small and V-shpaed, of moderate thickness, set well on the head, and dropping forward closely to the cheek. The top of the folded ear should be well above the level of the skull. The ear must be free of fringe, and the hair thereon shorter and darker in colour than the body.

Mouth. — The teeth should be even, strong and free from discoloration, the top teeth slightly overlapping the lower.

Neck. — Should be of a fair length and gradually widening towards the shoulders, well carried, and free of throatiness. There is generally a slight frill at each side of the neck, running nearly to the corner of the ear.

Forequarters. — The shoulders must be fine, long, and sloping well into the back. The legs moderately long, well set from the shoulders, perfectly straight, with plenty of bone and muscle; the elbows working freely clear of the sides; pasterns short and straight, hardly noticeable. The forelegs should be moved straight forward when travelling. The hair on the legs should be dense and crisp.

Body. — Chest deep and muscular, but neither full nor wide. Body moderately long; back should be strong and straight, with no appearance of slackness behind the shoulders; the loin muscular and slightly arched; ribs fairly sprung, rather deep than round, and well-ribbed back.

Hindquarters. — Should be strong and muscular, the thighs powerful, hocks near the ground, stifles moderately bent. The hind legs should be moved straight forward when travelling, the stifles not turned outwards. The hair on the legs should be dense and crisp.

Feet. — Should be strong tolerably round, and moderately small, toes arched, and neither turned out not in; black toe nails most desirable. Pads must be sound and free from cracks or horny excrescences.

Tail. — Generally docked to about three quarters; should be free of fringe or feather, but well covered with rough hair, set on pretty high, carried gaily, but not over the back or curled.

Coat. — Hard and wiry, having a broken appearance, free of softness or silkiness, not so long as to hide the outline of the body, particularly in the hindquarters, straight and flat, no shagginess and free of lock or curl. At the base of these stiff hairs is a growth of finer and softer hair, usually termed the undercoat.

Colour. — Should be "whole-coloured", the most preferable colours being a bright red, red wheaten, or yellow red. White sometimes appears on chest and feet and is more objectionable on the latter than on the former, as a speck of white on chest is frequently to be seen in all self-coloured breeds.

Weight and Size. — The most desirable weight in Show condition is, for a dog, 27 lbs., and for a bitch, 25 lbs. Height at shoulders, approximately 18 inches.

Note. — Male animals should have two apparently normal testicles fully descended into the scrotum.

IRISH TERRIER REGISTRATIONS 1981 — 87 INCLUSIVE

1981 — 139
1982 — 130
1983 — 146
1984 — 165
1985 — 184
1986 — 137
1987 — 135

YET TO WIN CRUFTS BEST-IN-SHOW.

KERRY BLUE TERRIER

The Kerry Blue Terrier is a tough, no nonsense dog in the finest terrier tradition.

Hailing from County Kerry in Eire, he has been used for a variety of useful jobs for many years. Among these tasks have geen guarding, small hunting and even herding sheep and cattle.

It was not until the early 1920's that England began to show interest in this fine breed and although he could not be called a common breed, he has made a good impact on the English show world and given great pleasure to many as a house pet.

Although he is the soul of good manners when in human company, the Kerry Blue is noted as a ferocious fighter with his own kind. This behaviour should naturally be discouraged from puppyhood, but total success in that endeavour would be difficult.

The Kerry Blue is an excellent guard dog and is of sufficiently solid proportions to discourage any unwanted visitor. He is easily house trained and does not shed any hairs although the dense coat does requre very frequent clipping.

Plenty of boisterous play and rigoroous exercise is enjoyed by this breed, so an elderly or infirm owner would not be advised.

KEY TO CHARACTER	
INTELLIGENCE	****
TEMPERAMENT	****
EASE OF COAT CARE	**
SUITABILITY FOR SMALL DWELLING	**
***** (5) = VERY GOOD	

BRITISH KENNEL CLUB STANDARD

KERRY BLUE TERRIER

CHARACTERISTICS. — Disciplined gameness. The Kerry Blue Terrier is a compact, powerful Terrier, showing gracefulness and an attitude of alert determination, with definite Terrier style and character throughout.

GENERAL APPEARANCE. — The typical Kerry Blue Terrier should be upstanding, well knit and well proportioned, showing a well-developed and muscular body.

Head and Skull. — Well balanced, long, proportionately lean, with slight stop and flat over the skull. Foreface and jaw very strong, deep and punishing; nose black; nostrils of due proportion.

Eyes. — Dark as possible. Small to medium with keen Terrier expression.

Ears. — Small to medium and V-shaped, carried forward but not as high as in some Terrier breeds.

Mouth. — Teeth level with upper teeth just closing over the lower; dark gums and roof.

Neck. — Strong and reachy, running into sloping sholders.

Forequarters. — Shoulders flat as possible with elbows carried close to the body while the dog is standing or in action. Legs straight, bone powerful. Front straight, neither too wide nor too narrow.

Body. — Short coupled with good depth of brisket and well sprung ribs. Chest to be deep. Topline level.

Hindquarters. — Large and well developed, stifle bent and hocks close to the ground giving perfect freedom of hind action.

Feet. — Round and small. Toe nails black.

Tail. — Set on high to complete a perfectly staight back and carried erect.

Coat. — Soft and silky, plentiful and wavy.

Colour. — Any shade of blue, with or without black points. A shade of tan is permissible in puppies, as is also a dark colour up to the age of 18 months. A small white patch on chest should not be penalised.

Weight and Size. — The most desirable weight for a fully-developed dog is from 33 to 37 lbs., and bitches should weigh proportionately less, but 35 lbs., is the most desirable weight to aim for. Ideal height: dogs 18 to 19 inches at shoulder; bitches slightly less.

Faults. — Hard or woolly coat. Solid black after 18 months. In excess of 19 inches in height. Bumpy cheek bones, teeth undershot or very overshot. Rose ears. Snipy foreface. Light-coloured or full eyes. Roach or hollowback. Close, stilted or cow-hocked hind action.

Note. — Male animals should have two apparently normal testicles fully descended into the scrotum.

MAIN AMERICAN KENNEL CLUB VARIATION TO STANDARD FOR THE KETTY BLUE TERRIER —

Height. — The ideal Kerry should be 18½ inches at the withers for a dog, slightly less for a bitch.

Weight. — The most desirable weight for a fully developed dog is from 33 to 40 pounds, bitches weighing proportionately less.

KERRY BLUE TERRIER REGISTRATIONS 1981 — 87 INCLUSIVE

1981 — 260
1982 — 299
1983 — 305
1984 — 302
1985 — 316
1986 — 315
1987 — 256

CRUFTS BEST-IN-SHOW WINNER.

1979 ENG. AM. CH. CALLAGHAN OF LEANDER — MRS W. STREATFIELD.

LAKELAND TERRIER

This tough, energetic terrier originated in the Lake District and was officially registered in 1921. Before then there had been several varieties of Terrier in the area, each named after it's particular region. All these dogs, though, were of similar type and all were used for fox hunting as they were very adept at burrowing in the difficult Lakeland terrain. Various owners of these Terrier packs eventually formed a Lakeland Terrier club and from then onwards there has been but one distinct variety.

Although only a moderately popular Terrier, the Lakeland has won his fair share of top show honours. When trimmed by an expert and presented in prime condition, he can be the epitome of smartness. The coat can come in any of several colour schemes and this adds to the interest created by the breed amongst Terrier enthusiasts.

The Lakeland Terrier has all the classic Terrier features of gameness, high spirits and love of human company. He is a manageable size for almost any home and his sharp bark is sufficient to discourage any would-be intruder.

This breed possesses great stamina and loves vigorous exercise, this provision being made, the Lakeland makes a fine companion.

```
┌─────────────────────────────────────────────────────┐
│                  KEY TO CHARACTER                     │
├─────────────────────────────────────────────────────┤
│  INTELLIGENCE              ***                         │
│                                                       │
│  TEMPERAMENT               ****                        │
│                                                       │
│  EASE OF COAT CARE         ***                         │
│                                                       │
│  SUITABILITY FOR           ****                        │
│  SMALL DWELLING                                        │
├─────────────────────────────────────────────────────┤
│              ***** (5) = VERY GOOD                    │
└─────────────────────────────────────────────────────┘
```

BRITISH KENNEL CLUB STANDARD

LAKELAND TERRIER

GENERAL APPEARANCE. — Smart and workman-like, with gay fearless demeanour.

Head and Skull. — Well balanced. Skull flat and refined. The jaws powerful and the muzzle should be broad but not too long. The length of the head from the stop to the tip of the nose should not exceed that from the occiput to the stop. Nose black.

Eyes. — Should be dark or hazel.

Ears. — Moderately small, V-shaped and carried alertly. They should not be placed too high or too low on the head.

Mouth. — Teeth even, closing scissor fashion, i.e., top teeth fitting closely over lower.

Neck. — Reachy.

Forequarters. — Shoulders well laid back. Forelegs straight, well boned.

Body. — Chest reasonably narrow. Back strong, moderately short, well coupled.

Hindquarters. — Strong and muscular, thighs long and powerful, well turned stifles, hocks low to ground and straight.

Feet. — Small, compact, round and well padded.

Tail. — Well set on, carried gaily but not to curl over the back.

Coat. — Dense and weather resisting, harsh with good undercoat.

Colour. — Black and tan, blue and tan, red, wheaten, red grizzle, liver, blue or black. Small tips of white on feet and chest not to debar. Mahogany or deep tan is not typical.

Weight and Size. — The average weight of dogs is 17 lbs., bitches 15 lbs. The height should not exceed 14½ inches at the shoulder.

Faults. — A true Lakeland Terrier expression is determined by head, ears and eyes. Too long a head, ears set on the top of the head, and slanting eyes are faults.

Note. — Male animals should have two apparently normal testicles fully descended into the scrotum.

MAIN AMERICAN KENNEL CLUB VARIATION TO STANDARD FOR THE LAKELAND TERRIER —

Size. — The ideal height of the mature dog is 14½ inches from the withers to the ground, with up to a ½ inch deviation either way permissible. Bitches may measure as much as one inch less than dogs. The weight of the well-balanced, mature specimen in hard, show condition, averages approximately 17 pounds, those of other heights proportionately more or less.

LAKELAND TERRIER REGISTRATIONS 1981 — 87 INCLUSIVE

1981 — 273
1982 — 268
1983 — 270
1984 — 303
1985 — 292
1986 — 236
1987 — 257

CRUFTS BEST-IN-SHOW WINNER TWICE.

1963 ROGERHOLM RECRUIT — W. ROGERS
1967 CH. STINGRAY OF DERRYABAH — MR & MRS W. POSTLEWAITE.

MANCHESTER TERRIER

The spirited Manchester Terrier descends directly from the old Black and Tan Terriers that were once common in nothern England. These hardy little dogs were principally used for ratting and their skill at this work was reputed to be unsurpassed. In fact their prowess was such that a grisly form of entertainment known as the 'rat pit' flourished among working men. At these events dozens of rats would be released in a pit and a Black and Tan Terrier would be thrown amongst them. Bets were taken on how quickly the dog would kill a given number of rats.

A crossing of one of these rather coarse dogs with a Whippet is thought to have laid the foundations of today's Manchester Terrier. The ealry dogs would often vary greatly in size and when they were first exhibited at dog shows there were two distinct weight categories. Both these types were bracketed as Black and Tan Terriers but over a century ago the two were given the distinct titles of English Toy Terrier for the smaller and Manchester Terrier for the larger.

Although not a widespread breed by any means, the Manchester Terrier has many fine attributes. In the home he is extremely clean, has no odour and is of an uncomplaining and unfussy disposition. He enjoys human company and makes a tireless and friendly playmate for children. The sleek coat and appealing markings make this an attractive small dog and he will maintain his well-being on only a moderate amount of exercise.

KEY TO CHARACTER	
INTELLIGENCE	***
TEMPERAMENT	****
EASE OF COAT CARE	*****
SUITABILITY FOR SMALL DWELLING	*****
***** (5) = VERY GOOD	

BRITISH KENNEL CLUB STANDARD

MANCHESTER TERRIER

GENERAL APPEARANCE. — The dog shall be compact in appearance with good bone and free from any resemblance to the Whippet.

Head and Skull. — Long, flat in skull and narrow, level and wedge-shaped, without showing cheek muscles; well-filled up under the eyes, with tapering, tight lipped jaws.

Eyes. — Small, dark and sparkling, oblong in shape, set close in head, not prominent.

Ears. — Small and V-shaped, carried well above the top line of the head and hanging to the head above the eyes.

Mouth. — Should be level.

Neck. — The neck should be fairly long and tapering from the shoulder to the head and slightly arched at the crest, free from throatiness.

Forequarters. — The shoulders should be clean and well sloped. The chest narrow and deep. The forelegs must be quite straight, set on well under the dog; and of proportionate length to the body.

Body. — Short with well-sprung ribs, slightly roached and well cut up behind the ribs.

Hindquarters. — The hind legs should be neigher cow-hocked nor with the feet turned in and well bent at the stifle.

Feet. — Small, semi-harefooted, and strong with well-arched toes.

Tail. — Short and set on where the arch of the back ends, thick where it joins the body and tapering to a point, carried not higher than the level of the back.

Coat. — Close, smooth, short and glossy, of a firm texture.

Colour. — Jet black and rich mahogany tan distributed as follows: on the head, the muzzle to be tanned to the nose, the nose and nasal bone to be jet black. There shall be a small tan spot on each cheek and above each eye, the under-jaw and throat to be tanned with a distinct tan V. The legs from the knee downward to be tanned with the exception of the toes which shall be pencilled with black, and a distinct black mark (thumb mark) immediately above the feet. Inside the hind legs tanned but divided with black at the stifle joint. Under the tail tanned, the vent tanned but as narrow as possible so that it is covered by the tail. A slight tan mark on each side of the chest. Tan outside the hind legs, commonly called breeching, a defect. In all cases the black should not run into the tan or vice versa, but the division between the colours shall be clearly defined.

Weight and Size. — Desired height at shoulders 16 inches dogs, 15 inches bitches.

Note. — Male animals should have two apparently normal testicles fully descended into the scrotum.

MAIN AMERICAN KENNEL CLUB VARIATION TO STANDARD FOR THE MANCHESTER TERRIER —

Weith. — Over 12 pounds and not exceeding 22 pounds.

Ears. — Erect, or button, small and thin; smaller at the root and set as close together as possible at the top of the head. If cropped, to a point, long and carried erect.

MANCHESTER TERRIER REGISTRATIONS 1981 — 87 INCLUSIVE

1981 — 91
1982 — 102
1983 — 160
1984 — 135
1985 — 186
1986 — 160
1987 — 103

YET TO WIN CRUFTS BEST-IN-SHOW.

NORFOLK TERRIER

The Norfolk Terrier existed in similar form for many years under te same title as today's Norwich Terrier. It was only in 1964 that he became a fully-fledged breed in his own right. The only marked difference between the two is still the ears, the Norwich having erect, pointed ears.

He has always been used for hunting and has the sturdiness and strong character that such work often requires. His short but powerful legs are ideal for digging after badgers and foxes and the hard coat serves as good protection from the weather and from the hazards of thorns and the like.

Being almost identical to his fellow East Anglian, he too shares the friendly nature of the Norwich. He enjoys being with children and makes a fine playmate for them. Given plenty of attention and regular exercise he makes a rewarding addition to any family who want a small but unfussy dog.

```
┌─────────────────────────────────────────────────────────┐
│                    KEY TO CHARACTER                       │
├─────────────────────────────────────────────────────────┤
│  INTELLIGENCE              ***                            │
│                                                           │
│  TEMPERAMENT              ****                            │
│                                                           │
│  EASE OF COAT CARE        ****                            │
│                                                           │
│  SUITABILITY FOR          *****                           │
│  SMALL DWELLING                                           │
├─────────────────────────────────────────────────────────┤
│              ***** (5) = VERY GOOD                        │
└─────────────────────────────────────────────────────────┘
```

BRITISH KENNEL CLUB STANDARD

NORFOLK TERRIER

CHARACTERISTICS. — The Norfolk Terrier is one of the smallest of the Terriers, but a "demon" for its size. Of a lovable disposition, not quarrelsome, with a hardy constitution. Temperament: Alert and fearless.

GENERAL APPEARANCE. — A small low keen dog, compact and strong with short back, good substance and bone. Honourable scars from fair wear and tear should not be penalised unduly.

Head and Skull. — Skull wide and slightly rounded with good width between the ears. Muzzle wedge-shaped and strong; length of muzzle slightly less than half the length of skull. Stop should be well defined.

Eyes. — Oval shaped and deep set, in colour dark brown or black. Expression alert, keen and intelligent.

Ears. — Size medium "V"-shaped but slightly rounded at tip, dropping forward close to the cheek.

Mouth. — Tight lipped, jaw strong; teeth strong and rather large; scissor bite.

Neck. — Medium length and strong.

Forequarters. — Clean and powerful shoulders with short powerful and straight legs.

Body. — Compact with short back, level topline, well sprung ribs.

Hindquarters. — Well muscled, good turn of stifle, hocks well let down and straight when viewed from rear; with great powers of propulsion.

Feet. — Round with thick pads.

Tail. — Medium docked, not excessively gay.

Coat. — Hard, wiry and straight, lying close to the body. It is longer and rougher on the neck and shoulders. Hair on head and ears short and smooth, except for slight whiskers and eyebrows.

Colour. — All shades of red, red wheaten, black and tan or grizzle. White marks or patches are undesirable but shall not disqualify.

Size. — Ideal height 10 in. at withers.

Faults. — Any departure from the foregoing points should be considered a fault and the seriousness of the fault should be in exact proportion to its degree.

Note. — Male animals should have two apparently normal testicles fully descended into the scrotum.

MAIN AMERICAN KENNEL CLUB VARIATION TO STANDARD FOR THE NORFOLK TERRIER —

Size. — Height at the withers 9 to 10 inches at maturity. Bitches tend to be smaller than dogs. Weight 11 to 12 pounds or that which is suitable for each individual dog's structure and balance.

NORFOLK TERRIER REGISTRATIONS 1981 — 87 INCLUSIVE

1981 — 272
1982 — 302
1983 — 295
1984 — 316
1985 — 360
1986 — 349
1987 — 398

YET TO WIN CRUFTS BEST-IN-SHOW.

NORWICH TERRIER

The beginnings of this fine Terrier go back to the mid-nineteenth century. Small short-legged Terriers were used for hunting fox and badger at that time in East Anglia and the courage and hardness of these dogs was renowned. They also gained favour amongst Cambridge students who used to hunt vermin and small game with them as a means of recreation. The small size of these Terriers enabling the undergraduates to keep them in their rooms.

Most credit for the development of the Norwich Terrier we see today goes to a breeder called Jones. He crossed local dogs with Glen of Imaal and Irish Terriers, the resulting breed taking it's name from the breeder. These 'Jones' Terriers were possibly the first modern Norwich-types.

Until 1964 Norwich Terriers had existed in two forms, the prick-eared and the drop-eared. But demand grew from followers of each variety for a separating of the two. the new standard for the Norwich was then drawn up and the two breeds have been kept pure ever since, the Norfolk, therefore being a relatively new distinct breed.

He is a very manageable and good-tempered little dog to have around the home and he revels in human attention from all age groups. He is full of spirit and due to his hunting past will love to chase anything that moves. Exercise should consist of regular walks at least and he will enjoy running free in the countryside whenever possible.

KEY TO CHARACTER	
INTELLIGENCE	***
TEMPERAMENT	****
EASE OF COAT CARE	****
SUITABILITY FOR SMALL DWELLING	*****
***** (5) = VERY GOOD	

BRITISH KENNEL CLUB STANDARD

NORWICH TERRIER

CHARACTERISTICS. — The Norwich Terrier is one of the smallest of the terriers. Of a lovable disposition, not quarrelsome, tremendously active and with a hardy constitution. Temperament gay and fearless.

GENERAL APPEARANCE. — A small, low, keen dog, compact and strong with good substance and bone. Honourable scars from fair wear and tear should not be penalised unduly.

Head and Skull. — Muzzle wedge-shaped and strong; length about one third less than a measurement form the occiput to the bottom of the stop, which should be well defined. Skull wide, good width between the ears, and slightly rounded.

Eyes. — Small and oval shaped, dark, full of expression, bright and keen.

Ears. — Erect, set well apart on top of skull. Of medium size with pointed tips. Held perfectly erect when aroused. Can be laid back when not at attention.

Mouth. — Tight lipped, jaws clean and strong. Teeth strong, rather large. Scissor bite.

Neck. — Neck strong of good length, commensurate with correct overall balance, flowing into well laid back shoulders.

Forequarters. — Legs short, powerful and straight; elbows close to body. Pasterns firm and upright. Legs should be moving straight forward when travelling.

Body. — Short back, compact body with good depth. Rib cage should be long and well sprung with short loin. Level topline.

Hindquarters. — Broad, strong and muscular, with well turned stifle. Low set hock with great powers of propulsion. Hind legs should follow in the track of the forelegs when moving, showing the pads and with hocks parallel.

Feet. — Round, well padded and catlike. To point straight forward standing and moving.

Tail. — Medium docked. Set on high to complete a perfectly level topline. Carried erect.

Coat. — Hard, wiry and straight, lying close to the body with a thick undercoat. Longer and rougher on the neck forming a ruff to frame the face. Hair on head and ears short and smooth, except for slight whiskers and eyebrows.

Colour. — All shades of red, wheaten, black and tan, or grizzle. White marks or patches are undesirable.

Size. — Ideal height 10 inches (25.4cm) at withers. This ideal height should not be attained by excessive length of leg.

Faults. — Any departure form the foregoing points should be considered a fault and the seriousness of the fault should be in exact proportion to its degree.

Note. — Male animals should have two apparently normal testicles fully descended into the scrotum.

NORWICH TERRIER REGISTRATIONS 1981 — 87 INCLUSIVE

1981 — 117
1982 — 135
1983 — 114
1984 — 131
1985 — 121
1986 — 165
1987 — 142

YET TO WIN CRUFTS BEST-IN-SHOW.

SCOTTISH TERRIER

There have been various strains of Terrier in Scotland for many centuries and accurate records of them are scarce. It seems though, that the Scottish Terrier descends from dogs that were used to hunt vermin and small game in the Perthshire region. Although the breed was not officially registered until 1879, he existed in a smilar form for many years before then.

Many of the early Terriers from Scotland became known simply as Scottish Terriers but since many of them resembled Cairn Terriers, Sky Terriers and others, this led to extreme confusion among the dog fanciers of the 19th century. But after much uncertainty and argument, a standardised version was agreed upon and the Scottish Terrier has gone on to become a very successful show dog and highly esteemed pet.

Sometimes called the Aberdeen Terrier, due to the famous efforts of early breeders in that city, this breed is one of the gamest terriers. His totally fearless approach to hunting has remained in his make-up to this day. He is generally very good natured and loves plenty of spirited play, but he will take no nonsense if teased or mistreated. Although black is by far the most common colour, wheaten and brindle specimens also occur. All of these colours can look very attactive if care is taken with grooming.

```
┌─────────────────────────────────────────────────────┐
│               KEY TO CHARACTER                       │
├─────────────────────────────────────────────────────┤
│  INTELLIGENCE                    ***                 │
│                                                      │
│  TEMPERAMENT                     ***                 │
│                                                      │
│  EASE OF COAT CARE               **                  │
│                                                      │
│  SUITABILITY FOR                 *****               │
│  SMALL DWELLING                                      │
├─────────────────────────────────────────────────────┤
│           ***** (5) = VERY GOOD                      │
└─────────────────────────────────────────────────────┘
```

BRITISH KENNEL CLUB STANDARD

SCOTTISH TERRIER

GENERAL APPEARANCE. — A Scottish Terier is a sturdy thick-set dog of a suitable size to go to ground, placed on short legs, alert in carriage, and suggestive of great power and activity in small compass. The head gives the impression of being long for a dog of its size. The body is covered with a close-lying, broken, rough-textured coat; with its keen inteliigent eyes and sharp prick ears, the dog looks willing to go anywhere and do anything. In spite of its short legs, the construction is such that it is a very agile and active dog. The movement of the dog is smooth, easy, and straight forward, with free action at shoulder, stifle and hock.

Head and Skull. — Without being out of proportion to the size of the dog, it should be long, the length of skull enabling it to be fairly wide and yet retain a narrow appearance. The skull is nearly flat and the cheek-bones do not protrude. There is a slight, but distinct stop between skull and foreface just in front of the eye. The nose is large, and in profile the line from the nose towards the chin appears to slope backwards.

Eyes. — Should be almond-shaped, dark brown, fairly wide apart and set deeply under the eyebrows.

Ears. — Neat, of fine texture, pointed and erect.

Mouth. — The teeth large, the upper incisors closely overlapping the lower.

Neck. — Muscular, of moderate length.

Forequarters. — The head is carried on a muscular neck of moderate length, showing quality, set into a long sloping shoulder; the brisket well in front of the forelegs, which are straight and well-boned to straight pasterns. The chest fairly broad and hung between the forelegs, which must not be out at elbows nor placed under the body.

Body. — The body has well-rounded ribs, which flatten to a deep chest and are carried well back. The back is proportionately short and very muscular. In general the top line of the body should be straight and level; the loin muscular and deep, thus powerfully coupling the ribs to the hindquarters.

Hindquarters. — Remarkably powerful for the size of the dog. Big and wide buttocks. Thighs deep and muscular, well bent at stifle. Hocks strong and well bent and turned neither inwards nor outwards.

Feet. — Of good size and well padded, toes well arched and close-knit.

Tail. — Of moderate length to give a general balance to the dog, thick at the root and tapering towards the tip, set on with an upright carriage or with a slight bend.

Coat. — The dog has two coats, the undercoat short, dense, and soft; the outer coat harsh, dense, and wiry; the two making a weather-resisting covering to the dog.

Colour. — Black, wheaten or brindle of any colour.

Weight and Size. — The ideally-made dog in hard show condition should weigh from 19 lbs. to 23 lbs. Height, 10 to 11 inches.

Note. — Male animals should have two apparently normal testicles fully descended into the scrotum.

MAIN AMERICAN KENNEL CLUB VARIATION TO STANDARD FOR THE SCOTTISH TERRIER —

Size and Weight. — Height at the shoulder for either sex should be about 10 inches. Generally, a well-balanced Scottish Terrier dog of correct size should weigh from 19 to 22 pounds and a bitch, from 18 to 21 pounds.

SCOTTISH TERRIER REGISTRATIONS 1981 — 87 INCLUSIVE

1981 —   904
1982 —   849
1983 —   882
1984 —   961
1985 —   853
1986 —   902
1987 — 1009

CRUFTS BEST-IN-SHOW WINNER.

1929 HEATHER NECESSITY — E. CHAPMAN.

SEALYHAM TERRIER

The Sealyham Terrier was developed in Pembrokeshire during the latter part of the nineteenth century.

The town of Sealyham just outside Haverfordwest gave the breed it's name. Around this region the hunting men of the time worked to obtain the ideal terrier for hunting small game, particularly the badger. The dogs used in this quest were an interesting cocktail of personalities. The Welsh Corgi, Cheshire Terrier which was a small Bull Terrier type, Fox Terrier and Dandie Dinmont Terrier were all introduced in varying degrees. Early results were not always consistent, some dogs being barely similar to todays Sealyham, but the general pattern was set, sturdy, short-legged physique, strong jaws, mainly white coat and boundless courage and tenacity.

The breed was eventually registered in 1910 and became fairly popular between the two world wars, but numbers have slowly declined ever since. This, however, ensures a purer breed and todays Sealyham is surely one of the most striking terriers.

Firm, careful handling is essential with the Sealyham puppy as there can be a streak of bad temper in his character, which should not be allowed to flourish. Most, however, are playful and manageable with a good guarding instinct.

The coat can look very unsightly if not constantly cared for, so a prospective owner should be prepared for a daily grooming. Exercise must be frequent and fairly energetic.

KEY TO CHARACTER	
INTELLIGENCE	***
TEMPERAMENT	***
EASE OF COAT CARE	**
SUITABILITY FOR SMALL DWELLING	*****
***** (5) = VERY GOOD	

BRITISH KENNEL CLUB STANDARD

SEALYHAM TERRIER

CHARACTERISTICS. — Alert and fearless but of friendly dispositon.

GENERAL APPEARANCE. — Should be that of a freely moving and active dog, presenting a balanced picture of great substance in a small compass. General outline oblong, not square.

Head and Skull. — The skull slightly domed and wide between the ears. Cheek bones should not be prominent. Punishing square jaw, powerful and long. Nose black.

Eyes. — Dark, deep set, oval but not small. Unpigmented eye rims permissible.

Ears. — Size medium, slightly rounded at tip, and carried at side of cheek.

Mouth. — Teeth level and strong, with canine teeth fitting well into each other, and long for the size of the dog. A scissor bite is preferred viz the jaws should be strong, with a perfect, regular and complete scissor bite i.e., the upper teeth closely overlapping the lower teeth and set square to the jaws. A level bite is permissible.

Neck. — Fairly long, thick and muscular, on well-laid shoulders.

Forequarters. — Forelegs should be short, strong and as straight as possible consistent with the chest being well let down. Point of shoulder should be in line with point of elbow which should be close to side of chest.

Body. — Medium length, level and flexible with ribs well sprung. Chest broad and deep, well let down between forelegs.

Hindquarters. — Notably powerful for size of dog. Thighs deep and muscular with well bent stifle. Hocks strong, well bent and parallel to each other.

Feet. — Round and cat-like with thick pads. Feet pointing directly forward.

Gait. — Brisk and vigorous with plenty of drive.

Tail. — Set in line with back and carried erect. Quarters should protrude beyond set of tail.

Coat. — Long, hard and wiry topcoat with weather resistant under-coat.

Colour. — All white, or white with lemon, brown or badger pied markings on head and ears. Much black and heavy ticking undesirable.

Weight and Size. — Ideal weight: Dogs about 9Kg (20 lbs); Bitches about 8.2Kg (18 lbs). Height should not exceed 31cm (12″) at the shoulder. General conformation, overall balance, type and substance are the main criteria.

Faults. — Any departure from the foregoing points should be considered a fault and the seriousness with which the fault should be regarded should be in exact proportion to its degree.

Note. — Male animals should have two apparently normal testicles fully descended into the scrotum.

MAIN AMERICAN KENNEL CLUB VARIATION TO STANDARD FOR THE SEALYHAM TERRIER —

Height. — At withers about 10½ inches.

Weight. — 23 to 24 pounds for dogs; bitches slightly less. It should be borne in mind that size is more important than weight.

SEALYHAM TERRIER REGISTRATIONS 1981 — 87 INCLUSIVE

1981 — 140
1982 — 123
1983 — 107
1984 — 114
1985 — 63
1986 — 116
1987 — 86

YET TO WIN CRUFTS BEST-IN-SHOW.

SKYE TERRIER

Many Terriers of varying shape, size and character have been
known throughout Scotland for centuries. The same can be said
for the islands off the Scottish coast, Skye being one of these.
There is no hard evidence as to how the Skye Terrier first
appeared, most suggestions being based on folklore rather than
fact. It is known that he was always a valued hunter being used
mainly for badger, otter and fox and it seems from ancient
writings that in essence he has changed very little over the years.
He still has the short muscular legs, weatherproof coat and strong
jaws that stood his ancestors in good stead in the harsh
environment of their homeland.

Although far from the most popular of the Terriers, the Skye
makes a fine show dog and devoted companion. He is quite a
substantial dog and if the coat is well prepared and he is handled
skilfully then he makes an impressive sight in the show-ring. He is
to be seen in a variety of interesting colours which also adds
appeal. In the U.S.A. he was once an extremely popular breed
for showing and he is still very much in evidence there.

The Skye Terrier is very loyal to his master at all times and he
can be very cool with strangers. Generally, though, he is good-
natured and blends in well with a family. Plenty of outdoor
activity is needed as the Sky still has a lot of the hunter's energy
and stamina.

KEY TO CHARACTER	
INTELLIGENCE	***
TEMPERAMENT	****
EASE OF COAT CARE	*
SUITABILITY FOR SMALL DWELLING	***
***** (5) = VERY GOOD	

BRITISH KENNEL CLUB STANDARD

SKYE TERRIER

CHARACTERISTICS. — A one-man dog, distrustful of strangers but not vicious.

Head and Skull. — Head long with powerful jaws. Nose black.

Eyes. — Hazel, preferably dark brown, medium size, close set and full of expression.

Ears. — Prick or drop. When prick, gracefully feathered, not large, erect at outer edges and slanting towards each other at inner edge, from peak to skull. When drop, larger hanging straight, lying flat and close at front.

Mouth. — Teeth closing level.

Neck. — Long and slightly crested.

Forequarters. — Shoulders broad and close to body, chest deep. Legs short and muscular.

Body. — Long and low. Back level. Ribs well sprung, giving flattish appearance to sides. sides.

Hindquarters. — The hindquarters and flanks full and well developed. Legs short and muscular, no dew claws.

Feet. — Large and pointing forward.

Tail. — When hanging, upper part pendulous and lower half thrown back in a curve. When raised, a prolongation of the incline of the back, not raising higher nor curling up.

Coat. — Double. Under-coat short, close, soft and woolly. Overcoat long, hard, straight, flat and free from crisp and curl. Hair on head shorter, softer, veiling forehead and eyes. On ears overhanging inside, falling down and mingling with side locks, surrounding the ears like a fringe and allowing their shape to appear. Tail gracefully feathered.

Colour. — Dark or light grey, fawn, cream, black, with black points. In fact, any self colour allowing shading of the same colour and lighter undercoat, so long as the nose and ears are black. A small white spot on the chest is permissible.

Weight and Size. — Height 10 inches, total length 41½ inches, weight 25 lbs. Bitch, slightly smaller in same proportions.

Faults. — Yellow eyes, tail curled over back or any deformity.

Note. — Male animals should have two apparently normal testicles fully descended into the scrotum.

MAIN AMERICAN KENNEL CLUB VARIATION TO STANDARD FOR THE SKYE TERRIER —

Size. — Dogs: Shoulder height, 10 inches. Length, chest bone over tail at rump, 20 inches. Head, 8½ inches. Tail, 9 inches. Bitches: Shoulder height, 9½ inches. Length, chest bone over tail at rump, 19 inches. Head, 8 inches. Tail 8½ inches.

SKYE TERRIER REGISTRATIONS 1981 — 87 INCLUSIVE

1981 — 163
1982 — 100
1983 — 148
1984 — 103
1985 — 114
1986 — 110
1987 — 136

YET TO WIN CRUFTS BEST-IN-SHOW.

SOFT-COATED WHEATEN TERRIER

The Soft-Coated Wheaten Terrier is a truly Irish breed, not often seen outside his homeland. He is almost certainly the oldest of the breeds native to Ireland and under the abundant coat he bears a marked resemblance to another fine Irish terrier, the Kerry Blue. It is believed that these dogs share the same ancestry.

For centuries the Soft-Coated Wheaten has been used as an all purpose dog on the many small farms throughout Ireland. Breeding has been hap-hazard until this century and it was not until 1937 that the Irish Kennel Club officially recognised the breed.

Many Irish farmers would testify that the Soft-Coated Wheaten is a versatile and indispensable member of their family. He is a good ratter, can be used for herding and will fearlessly guard anything in his charge. They have slightly less natural aggression than many other terriers and are as fond of people as any breed.

In England and the U.S.A. the breed has made some headway but has not had the success that perhaps he deserves.

He is a dog of high spirits who needs a good deal of vigorous exercise. An owner who prefers a natural, totally unspoilt breed will suit the Soft-Coated Wheaten. He can be easily house-trained and will show great devotion if treated well. An added attraction is that the coat does not shed.

KEY TO CHARACTER	
INTELLIGENCE	****
TEMPERAMENT	****
EASE OF COAT CARE	***
SUITABILITY FOR SMALL DWELLING	**
***** (5) = VERY GOOD	

BRITISH KENNEL CLUB STANDARD

SOFT-COATED WHEATEN TERRIER

CHARACTERISTICS. — The Soft-Coated Wheaten Terrier should be good tempered, spirited and game. Full of confidence and humour; a delightful, affectionate, intelligent companion. A natural terrier with strong sporting instincts, hardy and of strong constitution.

GENERAL APPEARANCE. — A medium-sized, compact, upstanding terrier well covered with a soft, wheaten coloured, natural coat that falls in loose curls or waves. An active, short-coupled dog, strong and well built; well balanced in structure and movement, not exaggerated in any way. Standing four square with head and tail up, giving the appearance of a happy dog, full of character.

Head and Skull. — Head moderately long and profusely covered with coat which should fall forward over the eyes. The skull, while not being coarse, should not be narrow. Skull flat and not too wide between the ears. The stop should be well defined and the cheek bones not prominent. The distance from the eyes to nose not longer, and preferably shorter, than the distance from the eye to the occiput. Jaws strong and punishing, muzzle square with no suggestion of snipiness. The top-line of the muzzle absolutely straight and parallel with skull. The nose should be black and large for the size of dog. Head in general, powerful without being coarse.

Eyes. — A clear bright dark hazel. Squarely set under a strong brow and of medium size, Eye rims black.

Ears. — V-shaped and folded at level of skull. The forward edge should drop down and slightly forward to lie closely along the cheek, the back edge standing slightly away from the side of the head. Thin, small to medium in size, covered with coat and with a fringe.

Mouth. — Teeth large. Bite scissors (the tips of the upper incisors should lie tightly in front of the lower incisors.) Overshot and undershot are equally objectionable. Lips tight and black.

Neck. — Moderately long, strong, muscular and slightly arched. Without throatiness. Gradually widening toward, and running cleanly into, the shoulders.

Forequarters. — Shoulders long, well laid back, and slope inwards from points to withers. Well knit in, fine, but muscular. Viewed from any angle, the forelegs perfectly straight. Good bone and muscle. Pasterns strong and springy. Chest moderately wide. Dew claws on the front legs may be removed.

Body. — Compact, with powerful short loins. Back strong and level. Ribs well sprung, without roundness, providing a deep chest with relatively short coupling. Length of back from point of withers to base of tail should measure about the same as, or slightly less than, from point of withers to ground. Male animals should have two apparently normal testicles fully descended into the scrotum.

Hindquarters. — Thighs strong and muscular. Hindlegs well developed with powerful muscle and well bent stifles. Hocks well let down and turning neither in nor out. Dew claws on the hind legs should be removed.

Feet. — Strong and compact, turned neither in nor out. Good depth of pad. Toenails black.

Gait. — Movement free, graceful and lively. Well co-ordinated with long, low strides. Having reach in front and good drive behind; straight action fore and aft. The head and tail should be carried high, the backline remaining level.

Tail. — Docked. The tail of the fully grown dog should be about 4 to 5 inches long. Set on high, carried gaily, but never over the back. Not curled and not too thick.

Coat. — Soft and silky. Neither woolly nor wiry. Loosely waved or curly, but if curly, the curls should be large, light and loose. The coat should not stand off but should flow and fall naturally. The coat should be abundant all over the body and escpecially profuse on the head and legs. The length of the leg coat should be sufficient to give good balance to the length of coat on the head and body. There is no seasonal change in the length or texture of the mature coat. The Soft-Coated Wheaten Terrier is a natural dog and should so appear. Dogs that appear to be over trimmed or stylized should be penalised. For show purposes the coat may be tidied up to present a neat outline. Coat colour and texture do not stabilize until about 18 months and should be given some latitude in young dogs.

Colour. — A good clear wheaten. A shade of ripening wheat. A white coat and a red coat are equally objectionable. Dark shading on the ears is not untypical. There is often a slight fluctuation in the intensity of colour in the mature coat, but the overall effect should be light wheaten. Dark overall colour and the even darker markings often present in the immature coat clear by about 18 months, if not before.

Weight and Size. — Height: Dogs approximately 18 to 19½ inches measured at the withers. Bitches slightly less. Weight: Dogs approximately 35 to 45 pounds. Bitches somewhat less.

Faults. — Any departure from the foregoing points should be considered a fault and the seriousness of the fault should be in exact proportion to its degree.

MAIN AMERICAN KENNEL CLUB VARIATION TO STANDARD FOR THE SOFT-COATED WHEATEN TERRIER —

Size. — A dog shall be 18 to 19 inches at the withers, the ideal being 18½. A bitch shall be 17 to 18 inches at the withers, the ideal being 17½. dogs should weigh 35 to 40 pounds; bitches 30 to 35 pounds.

SOFT-COATED WHEATEN TERRIER REGISTRATIONS 1981 — 87 INCLUSIVE

1981 — 104
1982 — 89
1983 — 132
1984 — 141
1985 — 119
1986 — 148
1987 — 99

YET TO WIN CRUFTS BEST-IN-SHOW.

STAFFORDSHIRE BULL TERRIER

This powerful little dog came into being over 150 years ago. He was the result of crossing the Old English Bulldog with a Terrier of the period, the idea being to combine the brute strength of the Bulldog with the athleticism of the Terrier.

As well as being employed as a successful ratter, the Staffordshire Bull Terrier was the favourite breed amongst followers of the odious practice of organised dog fighting. Many dogs would be terribly injured or killed in these matches and a great deal of money was often wagered on the result. This appalling pastime has long since been banned, although it is sad to say that some illegal fights still take place.

The enormous agression of this breed is evident only when in combat with another dog and in the company of people there is no gentler breed. There is still an aura attached to the Saffordshire Bull Terrier and his bloody past and unfortunately some people seem to think it good for the ego to own a "ferocious" dog. This must surely be a poor reason for deciding upon a dog and an unworthy insult to such a fine breed.

He is well behaved in the home, but will be more manageable if given firm training as a puppy. He is extremely sociable and affectionate, especially with children. His boundless energy is best used up on frequent periods of exercise and this will keep his stocky physique in top condition.

KEY TO CHARACTER	
INTELLIGENCE	***
TEMPERAMENT	****
EASE OF COAT CARE	*****
SUITABILITY FOR SMALL DWELLING	***
***** (5) = VERY GOOD	

BRITISH KENNEL CLUB STANDARD

STAFFORDSHIRE BULL TERRIER

CHARACTERISTICS. — From the past history of the Staffordshire Bull Terrier, the modern dog draws his character of indomitable courage, high intelligence and tenacity. This coupled with his affection for his friends, and children in particular; his off-duty quietness and trustworthy stability, makes him the foremost all-purpose dog.

GENERAL APPEARANCE. — The Staffordshire Bull Terrier is a smooth coated dog. He should be of great strength for his size and although muscular, should be active and agile.

Head and Skull. — Short, deep through, broad skull, very pronounced cheek muscles, distinct stop, short foreface, black nose.

Eyes. — Dark preferable but may bear some relation to coat colour. Round, of medium size, and set to look straight ahead.

Ears. — Rose or half-pricked and not large. Full drop or prick to be penalised.

Mouth. — The mouth should be level, i.e., the incisors of the bottom jaw should fit closely inside the incisors of the top jaw, and the lips should be tight and clean. The badly undershot or overshot mouth to be heavily penalised.

Neck. — Muscular, rather short, clean in outline and gradually widening towards the shoulders.

Forequarters. — Legs straight and well-boned, set rather wide apart, without looseness at the shoulders, and showing no weakness at the pasterns, from which point the feet turn out a little.

Body. — The body should be close-coupled, with a level topline, wide front, deep brisket, well-sprung ribs and rather light in the loins.

Hindquarters. — The hindquarters should be well muscled, hocks let down with stifles well bent. Legs should be parallel when viewed from behind.

Feet. — The feet should be well padded, strong and of medium size.

Tail. — The tail should be of medium length, low set, tapering to a point and carried rather low. It should not curl much and may be likened to an old-fashioned pump handle.

Coat. — Smooth, short and close to the skin.

Colour. — Red, fawn, white, black or blue, or any of these colours with white. Any shade of brindle or any shade of brindle with white. Black-and-tan or liver-colour not to be encouraged.

Weight and Size. — Weight: Dogs, 28 lbs. to 38 lbs. Bitches, 24 lbs. to 34 lbs. Height (at shoulder), 14 to 16 inches, these heights being related to the weights.

Faults. — To be penalised in accordance with the severity of the fault:— Light eyes or pink eye-rims. Tail too long or badly curled. Non-conformation to the limits of weight or height. Full drop and prick ears. Undershot or overshot mouths. The following faults should debar a dog from winning any prize:— Pink (Dudley) nose. Badly undershot or overshot mouth. Badly undershot — where the lower jaw protrudes to such an extent that the incisors of the lower jaw do not touch those of the upper jaw. Badly overshot — where the upper jaw protrudes to such an extent that the incisors of the upper jaw do not touch those of the lower jaw.

Note. — Male animals should have two apparently normal testicles fully descended into the scrotum.

STAFFORDSHIRE BULL TERRIER REGISTRATIONS 1981 — 87 INCLUSIVE

1981 — 3374
1982 — 3968
1983 — 4709
1984 — 4809
1985 — 6419
1986 — 6473
1987 — 6233

YET TO WIN CRUFTS BEST-IN-SHOW.

WELSH TERRIER

Although only registered by the Kennel Club in 1886, dogs similar to today's Welsh Terrier had been known before then for more than a century. His most likely forebear was the old Black and Tan Terrier, a dog that was once widespread throughout Britain. The Welsh developed their own particular strain of this tough working breed and resisted any attempts to make him more like English Terriers.

The Welsh Terrier has always been used for hunting and he has the classic Terrier trademarks of stamina, great courage, strong jaw and sturdy legs for digging. He is know to be an adaptable hunter and will pursue all manner of small game in any weather.

The ease of handling, characteristic of this breed, is a great asset in the show-ring and he has a very keen if not enormous following in this field. He stands very well which the handler appreciates both in preparing his dog and when in actual competition.

The Welsh Terrier is an unfussy dog who combines even temperament with a love of play and mischief. He is of a nice, compact size, large enough to be quite an effective guard and small enough to be managed by an elderly owner. House-training should not be a great problem with this breed and generally he will be found to be a faithful and obedient companion. He will enjoy regular exercise, a good daily walk being the minimum requirement.

KEY TO CHARACTER	
INTELLIGENCE	***
TEMPERAMENT	****
EASE OF COAT CARE	***
SUITABILITY FOR SMALL DWELLING	****
***** (5) = VERY GOOD	

BRITISH KENNEL CLUB STANDARD

WELSH TERRIER

CHARACTERISTICS. — The Welsh Terrier is of a gay, volatile disposition and is rarely of a shy nature. He is affectionate, obedient and easily controlled, thus making him an eminently suitable dog for town life. His size and colour render him ideal as a house dog, as the former point is in his favour where accommodation is limited, whilst the latter feature precludes the necessity for frequent washing as in the case of a white terrier. He is game and fearless, but definitely not of a pugnacious disposition, although at all times able to hold his own when necessary. He is ideally constituted to be a perfect town or country companion. Welsh Terriers are normally hardy and of robust constitution, and need no pampering, whilst as working terriers they are second to none, being easily trained to all sorts of game and vermin to work with gun or ferrets, and are generally found to be capital water dogs.

Head and Skull. — The skull should be flat and rather wider between the ears than the Wire-Haired Fox Terrier. The jaw should be powerful, clean cut, rather deeper, and more punishing — giving the head a more masculine appearance than that usually seen on a Fox Terrier. Stop not too defined, fair length from stop to end of nose, the latter being of a black colour.

Eyes. — Should be small, well set in, of a dark colour, expressive and indicating abundant keenness. A round full eye is undesirable.

Ears. — Should be V-shaped, small, not too thin, set on fairly high, carried forward and close to the cheek.

Mouth. — Should be level with strong teeth.

Neck. — The neck should be of moderate length and thickness, slightly arched and sloping gracefully into the shoulders.

Forequarters. — The shoulders should be long, sloping and well set back. The legs should be straight and muscular, possessing ample bone, with upright and powerful pasterns.

Body. — The back should be short, and well ribbed up, the loin strong, good depth, and moderate width of chest.

Hindquarters. — Should be strong, thighs muscular, and of good length, with the hocks well bent, well let down and with ample bone.

Feet. — The feet should be small, round and catlike.

Tail. — The tail should be well set on, but not too gaily carried.

Coat. — Should be wiry, hard, very close and abundant. A single coat is undesirable.

Colour. — The colour should be black and tan for preference, or black grizzle and tan, free from black pencilling on toes. Black below the hocks is a fault.

Weight and Size. — The height at shoulder should not exceed 15½ inches. 20 to 21 lbs. shall be considered a fair average weight in working condition.

Faults. — A white, cheery or spotted nose. Prick, tulip or rose ears. An appreciable amount of black below the hocks.

Note. — Male animals should have two apparently normal testicles fully descended into the scrotum.

MAIN AMERICAN KENNEL CLUB VARIATION TO STANDARD FOR THE WELSH TERRIER —

Size. — Males are about 15 inches at withers, with an acceptable range between 15 and 15½ inches. Bitches may be proportionately smaller. Twenty pounds is considered an average weight, varying a few pounds depending on the height of the dog, and the density of bone.

WELSH TERRIER REGISTRATIONS 1981 — 87 INCLUSIVE

1981 — 272
1982 — 214
1983 — 251
1984 — 258
1985 — 259
1986 — 217
1987 — 201

CRUFTS BEST-IN-SHOW WINNER TWICE.

1951 TWYNSTAR DYMA-FI — CAPT. AND MRS I.M. THOMAS
1959 CH. SANDSTORM SARACEN — MESDAMES LEACH & THOMAS.

WEST HIGHLAND WHITE TERRIER

The West Highland White is deservedly one of the most popular terriers in Britain and has been in that position for a great many years.

It is probable that he is of the same descent as the Cairn Terrier and it is easy to see the similarities between the two. Like the Cairn, he is an ancient breed, similar dogs being known in Scotland some 400 years ago. There were various types of white terriers in the Highland regions and these were used as efficient working dogs on the bleak terrain thereabouts. They were unrivalled in their burrowing ability and their stubborness in the pursuit of rats, badgers and others and their white colouring made them easily visible on a murky winter's day.

In the 19th century there were two main strains of white Scottish terrier. These were the Poltalloch Terrier and the White Roseneath Terrier and they were the forerunners of todays West Highland White. Having been in evidence in one form or another for hundreds of years he finally was given official recognition by the Kennel Club in 1907.

Much of the Cairn Terrier's qualities are also to be found in the West Highland White, his closest relative. He requires only moderate grooming, is hardy and fearless, yet friendly and lively. Exercise is not as vital as with some breeds, but a daily walk and some energetic play will do much to maintain his good natured disposition.

KEY TO CHARACTER	
INTELLIGENCE	***
TEMPERAMENT	****
EASE OF COAT CARE	***
SUITABILITY FOR SMALL DWELLING	*****
***** (5) = VERY GOOD	

BRITISH KENNEL CLUB STANDARD

WEST HIGHLAND WHITE TERRIER

GENERAL APPEARANCE. — The general appearance of the West Hightland White Terrier is that of a small, game, hardy-looking Terrier, possessed of no small amount of self-esteem; with a varminty appearance; strongly built, deep in chest and back ribs; level back and powerful quarters on muscular legs, and exhibiting in a marked degree a great combination of strength and activity. Movement should be free, straight and easy all round. In the front the legs should be freely extended forward by the shoulder. The hind movement should be free, strong and close. The hocks should be freely flexed and drawn close in under the body, so that when moving off the foot, the body is pushed forward with some force. Stiff, stilted movement behind is very objectionable.

Head and Skull. — The skull should be slightly domed and when gripped across the forehead, should present a smooth contour. There should only be a very slight tapering from the skull at the level of the ears to the eyes. The distance from the occiput to the eyes should be slightly greater than the length of the foreface. The head should be thickly coated with hair, and carried at a right-angle or less, to the axis of the neck. On no account should the head be carried in the extended position. The foreface should gradually taper from the eye to the muzzle. There should be a distinct stop formed by heavy, bony ridges, immediately above and slightly overhanging the eye, and a slight indentation between the eyes. The foreface should not dish or fall away quickly below the eyes where it should be well made up. The jaws should be strong and level. The nose must be black. Should be fairly large, and forming a smooth contour with the rest of the muzzle. The nose must not project forward giving rise to a snipy appearance.

Eyes. — Should be widely set apart, medium in size, as dark as possible in colour, slightly sunk in head, sharp and intelligent, which, looking from under the heavy eyebrows, imparts a piercing look. Full or light-coloured eyes are objectionable.

Ears. — Small, erect and carried firmly, terminating in a sharp point. The hair on them should be short, smooth (velvety) and should not be cut. The ears should be free from any fringe at the top. Round pointed, broad, large or thick ears are very objectionable, also ears too heavily coated with hair.

Mouth. — Should be as broad between the canine teeth as is consistent with the sharp varminty expression required. The teeth should be large for the size of the dog, and should articulate in the following manner:— the lower canines should lock in front of the upper canines. There should be six teeth between the canines of the upper and lower incisors. The upper incisors should slightly overlap the lower incisors, the inner side of the upper incisors being in contact with the outer side of the lower incisors. There should be no appreciable space between the incisors when the mouth is closed ensuring a keen bite; a dead level mouth is not a fault.

Neck. — Should be sufficiently long to allow the proper set on of head required, muscular and gradually thickening towards the base allowing the neck to merge into nicely sloping shoulders, thus giving freedom of movement.

Forequarters. — The shoulders should be sloped backwards. The sholder blades should be broad and lie close to the chest wall. The joint formed by the shoulder blade and the upper arm should be placed forward, on account of the obliquity of the shoulder blades, bringing the elbows well in, and allowing the foreleg to move freely, parallel to the axis of the body, like the pendulum of a clock. Forelegs should be short and muscular, straight and thickly covered with short hard hair.

Body. — Compact. Back level, loins broad and strong. The chest should be deep and the ribs well arched in the upper half presenting a flattish side appearance. The back ribs should be of a considerable depth and the distance from the last rib of the quarters as short as is compatible with free movement of the body.

Hindquarters. — Strong, muscular and wide across the top. Legs should be short muscular and sinewy. The thighs very muscular and not too wide apart. The hocks bent and well set in under the body so as to be fairly close to each other when standing, walking or trotting. Cow-hocks detract from the general appearance. Straight or weak hocks are undesirable and are a fault.

Feet. — The forefeet are larger than the hind ones, are round, proportionate in size, strong, thickly padded and covered with short hard hair. The hind feet are smaller and thickly padded. The under-surface of the pads of feet and all nails should be preferably black.

Tail. — 5 to 6 inches long, covered with hard hair, no feather, as straight as possible, carried jauntily, not gay nor carried over the back. A long tail is objectionable and on no account should tails be docked.

Coat. —Colour pure white, must be doublecoated. The outer coat consists of hard hair, about 2 inches long, free from any curl. The under coat, which resembles fur, is short, soft and close. Open coats are objectionable.

Colour. — Pure white.

Weight and Size. — Size about 11 inches at the withers.

Note. — Male animals should have two apparently normal testicles fully descended into the scrotum.

WEST HIGHLAND WHITE TERRIER REGISTRATIONS 1981 — 87 INCLUSIVE

1981 — 3525
1982 — 3485
1983 —3950
1984 — 4153
1985 — 4864
1986 — 5155
1987 — 5339

CRUFTS BEST-IN-SHOW WINNER.

1976 CH. DIANTHUS BUTTONS — MRS K. NEWSTEAD.